AUTHORITY IN THE CHURCH

Authority in the Church

JOHN L. McKENZIE, S.J.

Sheed & Ward

© Sheed and Ward, Inc., 1966

Library of Congress Catalog Card Number 66-12270

ISBN: 0-934134-47-2

Imprimi potest:
   Very Rev. John R. Connery, S.J.
   Provincial
   Chicago Province of
   the Society of Jesus
   Feb. 23, 1966

Nihil obstat:
   Thomas J. Beary
   Censor Librorum

Imprimatur:
   ✝Robert F. Joyce
   Bishop of Burlington
   February 7, 1966

Sheed and Ward™ is a service of National Catholic Reporter Publishing, Inc.

Published by: Sheed and Ward
             P.O. Box 40292
             Kansas City, MO 64141

             800-821-7926

PREFACE

When the publisher made the somewhat chancy decision to reprint this book, I was asked for my approval and, if I approved the project, to write a preface for the reprinting. I first asked whether I should rewrite the entire book; and I was assured that this was not intended and, in fact, the printing schedule did not allow time for that.

At the time of this writing the late Philip Scharper, who suggested the idea of the book about 1964, has been dead only a few weeks. I need not add my voice to the many voices which have been raised in praise of this genial and thoroughly honest man, whose intellectual powers were as brilliant as the man was unassuming. I can do no more than dedicate the reprinting to his memory; the original printing had no dedication.

A couple of anecdotal memories of events since the first publication of this book may be of interest. I must notice that I have changed my residence seven times since 1965, when this book was written. In spite of the generous help of good friends in each move, for which I have never shown sufficient gratitude, there has been an inevitable growth of disorder and some erosion in the contents of my files. This means that while my memory is clear about events and personal identities, it is sometimes fuzzy about the sequence of events, dates and places. Remember that the Gospels were written from such memories. I shall try to exercise less freedom in the work of redaction than the writers of the Gospels did.

The book was published in 1966 with the Imprimatur of Bishop Joyce of Burlington. I do not know whether this book was partly responsible for a later crackdown by Rome on Bishop Joyce for operating too liberal a censorship of books in his diocese. In any case, the Roman instructions to Bishop Joyce on how to run his diocese illustrate very well the abuse of power about which I wrote. How many books published under Bishop Joyce's Imprimatur have even been officially condemned? As the next step in my narrative shows, it was not for lack of trying.

Sometime in early December 1967 I went to Washington to receive the Spellman award and medal from the American Catholic Theological Society. I think that his Eminence died the very night I received the award; as far as I know, his death was never attributed to the trauma of learning who was to receive the medal that year. Because of the illness of the Cardinal he was represented at the ceremony by two of his auxiliaries, Bishops Fearns and Cooke; the latter was only a few weeks away from acquiring a much higher profile. Either just before or just after the award was given — it seems inexcusable to forget the exact order of events — Archbishop Lucey of San Antonio denounced this book as heresy in a circular letter to his priests. Without any urging from me the Catholic Theological Association, then under the presidency of Walter Burghardt, an old friend, instituted an examination of the book, as much in its own interest as in mine. The board of examiners found the book as clean as a hound's tooth; but this happened later. At the moment I asked Robert Hoyt, of the NATIONAL CATHOLIC REPORTER, for space to respond to Lucey in the journal in which I first read the published news of Lucey's attack.

Space was graciously granted, and I wrote a letter in which I was no more insolent than the situation required. I concluded the letter by inviting the Archbishop to present his charges before ecclesiastical courts, which do exist, or shut up. Bob Hoyt, a more cautious editor than most people recognized, softened the last phrase for publication. This invitation was never accepted, either then or later, by the Archbishop or by any one else. It is probably safe to say that the orthodoxy of the book which you have in your hands has withstood more than the ordinary examinations to which manuscripts are submitted.

The last development in this story was made known to me by Phil Scharper some months later. Phil told me that some Roman Congregation (I never heard the name) had asked, urged or commanded that AUTHORITY IN THE CHURCH be removed from stock and from circulation and from production and from sales. Phil said that the company answered that without some good reason it was impossible to honor this request or command. As far as I know, this affair went no further.

It is not this experience alone, but my experience of the use of church authority in the last twenty years that has left me thinking on the eve of my seventy-fifth birthday that the Roman See (defined in the old Code of Canon Law as the complex of bureau and offices through which the Holy Father is accustomed to transact the business of the universal Church; cf. new Code Can. 361) is able to make dogmatic and disciplinary declarations for the whole Church, to impose obedience, submission and silence upon me and to enforce this imposition by all the legitimate means which it has in its power. The Roman See is not able to command respect from me; it can get respect only by deserving it. On rereading the book I was impressed by the cool rationality with which I could approach the subject in 1965. I doubt whether I could do so now; and since I would serve neither the welfare of the Church nor my own reputation by rewriting the book, I am quite ready to accept the reprinting in the original form.

June 11, 1985
Claremont, California   John L. McKenzie

Contents

AUTHORITY IN THE CHURCH

INTRODUCTION
The Nature of Authority

THE SECOND VATICAN COUNCIL has opened a number of issues which have been closed for years, even for generations. Comparisons of the Council to the ventilation of a room long closed and sealed have become routine; to carry the metaphor a little further, the admission of daylight has rendered visible a certain amount of disarray in the contents of the room and the deposits of dust which attest that objects have not been moved for a long time. By its actions the Council has stimulated theologians to study questions which they have long known ought to be studied, but for whose study the climate of opinion before the Council had not seemed favorable. Unless the movement of theology reverses itself, the Council will be followed by what the Church has needed for a few hundred years, a burst of creative theological thinking.

One of the areas which the Council has opened is the idea of authority in the Church. The Protestant revolt of the sixteenth century put Church authority on the defensive, and since that time this defensive posture has been no more than slightly modified. The posture was even hardened by the revolutionary movements in the intellectual and political worlds in the nineteenth century, and it was rendered rigid by the Modernist controversy at the opening of the twentieth century. It was an unfortunate if easily understood by-product of the Modernist controversy that the defensive posture of authority, previously turned against Protestant and agnostic groups, was turned against the members of the Church. The Church, it appeared, had unwittingly nursed vipers in its bosom, and measures were taken to assure beyond doubt that all the sons of the Church who were engaged in her governing and educational functions were legitimate. The test of legitimacy generally and practically was adherence to a theological structure which antedated Modernism. Generally and practically, I say, for it was not the intent and purpose of the pontifical document which dealt with Modernism to canonize the theology of the nineteenth century. The business of the Church is administered by men, however, and it is not surprising that men should form their policy and their decisions according to their interpretation of what the Church wishes. The weight of majority opinion fell on the side of pre-Modernist theology because no other place was known in which it could safely fall. There has, of course, been notable development in many areas of theology during the sixty years since the peak of the Modernist controversy. However, since in this controversy it was authority itself rather than any particular doctrinal area which seemed to be in question, theological development of the idea of authority has amounted to next to nothing.

The idea of ecclesiastical authority must be distinguished from the use of authority. There have been complaints in the Church about the use of authority at least since the epistles of Paul to the Corinthians. In all honesty, and as long as we limit the statement to a past which has left no survivors, we can say that these complaints were often legitimate. Some complaints were based on grounds which would be subject to complaint in any society. Authority in the Church has no more right to be unfair and imprudent than has any other authority, but it does not fail precisely as ecclesiastical authority when it exhibits such defects. Conversely, it does not succeed precisely as Church authority when it is fair and prudent; this minimum is expected of any authority. It is a different problem when complaints are based on an alleged deviation from the ideal of ecclesiastical authority as ecclesiastical. Criticism of this type and the responses to such criticism are based on a theoretical affirmation of what Church authority is. It is just in the area of theory that development has not kept pace with history.

One may have poor theory and good practice, or good theory and poor practice. Between the two those who are subject to authority will take the first over the second at any time they have a choice; but neither is an entirely satisfactory way of managing any business. Tension between theory and practice is avoided only by not thinking; and while not thinking may deaden the pain somewhat, it is not recommended as good operational practice on any but the lowest human level —the galley slave, for instance. Thought, that process which in Christian philosophy is the noblest and most godlike human operation, should not be suspended in the very fulfilment of the Christian ideal. If I did not believe that there is tension between theory and practice, I would not attempt to present any ideas on the subject. I believe there is and that we can locate the tension and move toward its relaxation.

It is natural to consider authority in the Church as a species of authority in general. It will be part of the thesis of this work that such a conception of authority is false to the New Testament idea of Church authority. This is said now as a preliminary; whether the proposition will stand or not must be left to the discussion which will follow in subsequent chapters. But in order to make the proposition clear and convincing, we shall have to consider authority in general and in other societies; only thus can we see how Church authority differs from other forms of authority. In the dictionary, authority is defined in its first meaning as the power or right to give commands, enforce obedience, take actions, or make final decisions; jurisdiction is given as a synonym. Jurisdiction is popularly but inaccurately used for authority in general; but jurisdiction is properly legal authority, both as legally constituted and as empowered to command by legislation. Jurisdiction as such is one species of authority, and we shall consider it in more detail. In the dictionary, "power" and "right" are used as if the two were synonymous, but they are not; right is moral power, resting on a moral basis which makes obedience morally good and disobedience morally bad. Power to command may be based on sheer superior force or on some form of moral coercion other than morally based authority; thus the commandant of a concentration camp or a blackmailer has the power to command, but in common language neither has authority. It follows that genuine obedience is rendered only to moral power, not to force or moral pressure. It follows also that the moral power of authority is not measured by the degree of control which it exercises. The line between the use of authority and tyranny is extremely thin, and it can be drawn only at the definition of power. Hannah Arendt has very precisely distinguished between authority and power and between authority and persuasion; she observes that, where force is used, authority has failed and, where arguments are used, authority is left in abeyance.[1]

Thomas Corbishley has defined the moral base of obedience in these terms:

Ideally, obedience is given naturally and almost spontaneously to the wise and good man, to the man whose authority is based on his power to see further, plan more effectively, conceive a nobler ideal than his subordinates. In principle, it is only in virtue of his possession of such qualities that obedience to him is justified. In

[1] *Between Past and Future* (New York: Viking Press, 1961), 91–141.

other words, obedience is a wholly rational and reasonable attitude of mind provided that the man who is in authority bases his orders on reason, on what is for the general good, which should be thought of as other than the good of the individuals constituting the general body.[2]

When we distinguish authority in the Church from authority in general, we shall find it difficult to omit any of the elements which Corbishley here includes. To paraphrase him briefly, the only moral base of the power of authority to command is that what authority commands is the right thing to do.

Authority exists in society and is based on the nature and the constitution of society. We do not have power first and then a society in which power may be exercised; first we have the society with its own end, and then authority as one of the means by which the end is achieved. "The right thing to do" is determined by the end of the society; when authority commands this, it has its full moral base, and disobedience attacks both the society and the end of the society. Since human beings are fallible and corruptible, a distinction arises between authority and the end of the society. Authority itself may act in opposition to the end of the society, and then disobedience rather than obedience becomes not only a right but a duty. Clear cases of this are rare; when they do occur, the right of the individual person to follow his own conscience must be maintained. Trouble arises more frequently when the decision of authority is open to reasonable doubt; in such instances, a reasonable general policy seems to be to give authority the benefit of the doubt. The consequences of disobedience, which does shake the structure of the society, must be weighed against the certainly presumed consequences of the action which authority intends. Reasonable doubts of this sort can be resolved only by completely candid consultation of the

[2] "Power and Authority," *The Way* 3(1963), 287–288.

members of the society by the authority; for it should not be reckoned that genuine obedience can be rendered with such a doubt.

Authority exists in the society and only for the society; and it loses its moral base if it deviates from the end of the society, whether by malice or by incompetence. John M. Todd has written:

At the creaturely level, this exchange of being, of possessions, of services, is the essential condition for the evolution of the individual person and of social life. The only legitimate human authority is that which favors this twofold evolution. Every authority which claims to go beyond this condition is tyrannical, is anarchy in reverse and bases personal and social life on falsehood and meaninglessness. 'Absolute' human power corrupts not only the man who commands but also the man who obeys, for the relations between the two cease to be human.[3]

In philosophy there are only two societies which are called natural: the family and the political society. All other societies are conventional, that is, they are created by men for a particular end which is not specified by human nature and the conditions of human existence. In conventional societies the basis of authority is contract; the authority is established by the mutual consent of those who form the society, and these are free also to determine the constitution of the society. The moral power to command in the family and the State is not based, in Christian ethics, on the consent of the members of the society; it is based on natural and universal human needs which can be met only by these societies antecedently to any contractual agreement. Every person must live in a family and a State just because he is a human person; membership in these societies is not a matter of personal choice. He must

[3] *Problems in Authority* (Baltimore: Helicon Press, 1962), 5.

accept these societies as cosmic principles which he has no power to remove or to alter essentially. That there are structural variations both in the family and in the State is obvious, but these variations are not under discussion. The important factor for our problem is that authority in the family and in the State reposes on a moral base which is prior to any human decision, individual or collective.

Family authority and political authority are as different from each other as the ends of the two societies are different; the authority of the family is called dominative, or paternal, and the authority of the State is called jurisdictional. The end of the family is the human fulfilment which husband and wife achieve by conjugal union and the rearing to maturity of the children born to them. Throughout human history most men have understood that the authority of the family rests in the father; modern Western society has come to think of dominative authority as held in partnership and does not consider the wife as subject to her husband in the same way that children are subject to their father. This change is an example of structural modification which does not affect the idea of authority itself. The authority of the family is directed to the maturation of the children; beyond this end the parents' use of their authority is left to their own wisdom and discretion, subject always to general moral principles. In ancient Roman law the father had the right of life and death over his children, and in many ancient societies as well as more recent primitive societies the father had the right to sustain the family by selling his children into slavery. In our ethics these practices are contrary to the end of dominative authority. But some moral restraints are found in every society; the term "dominative," applied to paternal authority, signifies that there are no restraints other than those imposed by the morality of the family and of society in general. No matter how unlimited dominative power may appear to be in some instances, it is always recognized as different from that type of authority over things which is called ownership.

The purpose of the political society is not the maturation of the citizens (or subjects), but "the common good," that social good which cannot be achieved by individuals as such. The common good in its minimum includes protection from external enemies and from internal corruption; in practice, this means the waging of war and the administration of law and justice. Modern governments have expanded the idea of the common good to include a large number of social services; again we see a structural modification which does not affect the idea of authority. The political society differs from the family in its power to govern by law, to administer law, and to exercise that kind of coercion which we call legal—concretely, the use of police power and of the courts; this is what is meant by jurisdiction. But law is also a restraint on political authority; by its laws the Government states to its citizens the terms within which it commands. Laws are subject to the ultimate end of the political society, the common good, which the Government must serve to maintain its moral power to govern.

Contractual associations, such as business concerns, universities and colleges, benevolent and fraternal associations—in a word, every society which is neither the family nor the State—yield in priority to both family and State. In modern Western culture free private associations must manage themselves according to the civil law which governs contracts and associations; and this law imposes rigid limitations on the authority within the conventional society which usually has no legal coercion other than expulsion from the society. In Christian ethics free private associations lack the moral base of command; it is not understood that those who form such private associations can communicate by contract either dominative or jurisdictional power. In these associations, however, the power of moral coercion can be very great—for instance, the power of employer over employee; and the use of moral coercion to a degree which exceeds the needs of the society is an abuse of power.

The moral base of authority makes obedience a morally good act. If authority loses its moral base, obedience ceases to be morally good. We have noticed that authority has no moral base except that what it commands is the right thing to do. Who determines that what authority commands is the right thing to do? If it is authority alone, then we have absolute power; what authority commands is right because it is commanded. If it is those under authority, then we seem to reduce society to a chaos of individual decisions. Since both conclusions are intolerable, we have no solution except to repose the judgment of the reasonableness of the command both in authority and in the governed. Whatever be the channels through which this common judgment is achieved, it can be said definitely that the society which has no means of reaching a common judgment is weak in its structure of authority. It is not to be imagined that authority loses its moral base every time it makes an error in judgment or allows malice to influence its decisions; but in sound theory it loses its power to command. Authority is sustained by the society in its weakness as authority sustains the members in their weakness; every society is composed of human beings, and it must tolerate the humanity of its components. But when authority habitually fails to command the right thing, it no longer serves the end of the society, and it cannot command the obedience of the governed. It must yield, voluntarily or involuntarily, to others who can bear authority worthily. Authority must maintain the moral base which the society gives it; it cannot rest upon itself as firmly established, whether it performs its work well or ill.

I said that it is an error to think of authority in the Church as a species of authority in general; even with this extremely brief survey of the species of authority, we are in a position to take the first step toward the thesis. For is the Church a political society with jurisdiction, or a family with dominative power, or a free contractual association? Plainly, it is none of the three, and therefore none of these species of power can be transferred to the Church. The Church has not as its end the common good which cannot be achieved by the members as individual persons. Dominative power does not belong to the Church, for, as Karl Rahner has observed, the purpose of dominative power is to bring its subjects to the point of maturity where they are no longer subject to dominative power. The Church is a free association in the sense that its members join by a free, personal decision; the Church is not a natural society in the sense that its constitution is determined by the human condition antecedently to any personal or collective action. Yet no one can seriously maintain that the authority of the Church is based on the contractual agreement of its members. If the Church differs from all these societies in its end and its means, authority in the Church will be determined to its reality by the end of the Church. Our purpose in this study will be to see how authority is related to the end of the Church in the New Testament.

The usual and canonical term for ecclesiastical authority in the Church is jurisdiction; indeed, this term was used in the definition of papal authority enunciated in the First Vatican Council. Obviously, no effort to get rid of this term can be mounted, and no such effort is envisaged here. But we shall have to notice that if we define jurisdiction in the Church in the terms in which jurisdiction is defined in the State, we shall have assimilated the Church to the State. It is an easy and not unattractive assimilation; if the scope of this study permitted —it does not—we might profit by examining, in some details, instances of this assimilation in the history of the Church.[4] This examination would show what can happen when authority in the Church is conceived in secular terms. We must, therefore, speak of jurisdiction in the Church as analogical to jurisdiction in the State, and not as univocal. It may seem to be a petty logical distinction, but it is of the highest importance here.

By a study of authority in the New Testament, by no means do I imply that the New Testament idea of authority is terminal, and that any development of the idea of authority beyond the New Testament is illegitimate. The theory of the development of doctrine has its place here; and the idea of authority is one of the better illustrations of the theory of development. As the Church has grown and moved with history and in history, it has had to produce new forms of authority and new uses of authority. There is nothing foreign to the nature of the Church in development as such; the Church could not respond to the demands of her mission did she not grow and adapt to changing needs. The continuity of the Church does not lie in fixity of forms and uses of authority, but in identity which is deeper than mere structure. There is no form of authority which is not open to abuse; but abuse does not take away the validity of the form.

Such development is a human process and is subject to human fault and failure. As we shall see, very few of the forms which authority takes in the modern Church have antecedents in the New Testament; evolution of form has been constant since the apostolic period. Weighed in the balance of history and theology, most of these forms appear to be phenomena which the Church produces and which the Church can take away. Some of them are better fitted to her mission,

---

[4] Yves Congar has sketched admirably the development of the idea of authority from the New Testament to the present in John M. Todd, *Problems in Authority*, 119–156.

and some less well fitted; some are suitable for certain periods
and cultures, and unsuited to others. Authority is indestruct-
ible and incorruptible in the Church; the concrete forms in
which authority appears do not share this incorruptibility.
The test of whether any particular form of authority is a
genuine development must ultimately be the New Testament,
for it is in this document that the original grant of authority
to the Church is seen. For this reason a study of authority in
the New Testament is always relevant for the Church; there
is no other way in which inner identity and continuity can
be perceived.

Far from being opposed to the idea of development, a study
of authority in the New Testament may indicate that development is arrested. In the contemporary Church, at least up to
the Second Vatican Council, this is not an idle question. I
have alluded to the defensive posture which the Church has
maintained since the sixteenth century. With reference to authority, the defensive posture has meant that many members
of the Church, particularly those who hold office, have been
tacitly unfavorable to any development of the idea of authority. The emphasis on obedience and due submission to
authority which we find in so many ecclesiastical statements,
both official and private, reflects the concern for the security
of authority which runs through the history of the Church
for the last four centuries. This concern is quite easy to explain historically. The Reformers rejected the authority of
the Church and withdrew themselves from its obedience. The
intellectual movement, called the Enlightenment, was regarded
as an attack on the Church and the faith; this judgment may
have been too hasty and severe, but the intellectuals of the
Enlightenment generally treated the teaching authority of the
Church as, at best, irrelevant to the advance of learning and,
at worst, as reactionary and obscurantist. In the eighteenth
and nineteenth centuries Church authority suffered staggering
blows from civil governments. A defensive posture was

adopted because there were so many points to be defended.

But excessive emphasis on any single feature of the life of the Church can obscure other features of that life. I hope to show in subsequent pages that the Christian life cannot be conceived in biblical terms as essentially a life of obedience and submission, but as something else in which obedience and submission have their place. The base of Christian obedience is not identical with the base of familial, or civic, or contractual obedience; unless statements on obedience make this clear, the faithful can think of the importance of Christian obedience in the same terms in which they think of the importance of secular obedience.

The absence of any development of the theory of authority during the last four hundred years has much to do with popular misconceptions of authority in the Church; and when I say "popular," I am not limiting these misconceptions to the laity. The adoption of the defensive posture meant that the idea of authority which was defended was frozen at the sixteenth-century stage of development. A full study of this phase of theology would take us beyond the scope of this study which is limited to the New Testament, and to my knowledge no such study has been made. It ought to be made. Such a study would show how the idea of authority, like so many elements in the external structure of the Church, is affected by the culture in which the Church exists and fulfills her mission. The position of the Church at any point of history is delicate. She must strike a nice balance between integration with secular culture and identification with secular culture. She must always avoid the two dangers of withdrawal from the culture and secularization; and in fact she rarely achieves this balance. The idea of authority in the Church is not the same as the idea of secular authority, and the danger of assimilation in this area is greater than it is in most others. A comparison of the use of authority in the Church in the sixteenth century with the social and political structures of Europe of the period would show to what an extent the use of authority was affected by the forms of secular authority.[5]

No specialized knowledge of medieval and Renaissance culture is necessary for one to see that the theory and the forms of secular authority in European society were absolute. No restraint on secular power was known except restraint imposed by another secular power or by the power of the Church. Church and State were conceived as two absolutes, each with no limitation within its sphere, and each was founded upon a divine mandate. The subject of a Renaissance prince could scarcely distinguish between the quality of the authority of his prince and the quality of the authority of his bishop. There was no appeal from one except to the other. Theoretically, the two divided temporal and spiritual authority between themselves; practically, since the two spheres are rationally and not really distinct in the persons whom the two ruled, the two powers were often at loggerheads. The temporal rule of the Pope over the Papal States did not clarify the matter. As prince of the Papal States, the Pope was as absolute a ruler as the Medicis in Florence; the absolute character of his temporal power was transferred to his spiritual power. Wherever the European looked at those who ruled him, whether in the Church or in the State, he thought of himself as a subject.

Political theory and practice in Europe and North America have evolved a long distance from the sixteenth-century State; and the political ideals of Western civilization have been exported to other continents, even though the countries of other continents have not yet shown themselves fully ready to make these ideals practical. To notice this evolution is not to imply that democracy is the best political form or that it is terminal; evolution will no doubt continue in politics—and evolution is

[5] Until a full study of the interaction of ecclesiastical and secular authority is made, one may usefully consult Ian McNeill, *Problems in Authority*, 157–167, and Patrick McGrath, *ibid.*, 168–176; Arthur Mirgeler, *Mutations of Western Christianity* (New York: Herder and Herder, 1964).

not synonymous with progress. The relevance of this political evolution to authority in the Church is that Western man no longer thinks of himself as a subject of the State, but as a citizen. He accepts Jefferson's principle that just governments derive their powers from the consent of the governed. He believes that the decisions of the State are his own decisions, at least through representative channels. The officers of the State are elected by him, and he can depose them. The people are sovereign, and the officers of State are responsible to the people. It has always been true that the government which was opposed to the popular will could not survive; but the popular will has channels of expression in modern democracy which it did not have four hundred years ago. Any modern government at least pretends to consult its citizens. The citizen of the modern democratic State thinks of himself as a part of the government, not as its subject.

This means that the modern Catholic does not look on his Church and his State as the same type of authority. There has been no development in the theory of authority in the Church to correspond to the political evolution of recent centuries. Likewise, there has been no evolution of the forms of authority in the Church; the Roman and diocesan offices are still organized as the staffs of absolute rulers. The theoretical lag is compensated to some extent by the discord between theory and practice, but when one compares the freedom exercised by subordinates in the fifteenth and sixteenth centuries with the tight discipline of the modern Church, one wonders whether theory and practice are not better integrated now than they were then. The use of authority now, I think, would have to be designated as absolute rather than as democratic, if we are forced to choose between the two words.

It will be part of our task in the pages that follow to show that authority is viewed in the New Testament neither as absolute nor as democratic, but unique in character. Nor is it our purpose, as I have said above, to suggest that the evolution of

Church authority should stop with the New Testament. But if evolution should not stop with the apostolic age, neither should it stop with the sixteenth century. One suspects that theological development of the theory of authority is regarded as an attack upon authority, subtle or open. Statements on the idea and use of authority quite often recall the members of the Church to an ideal of obedience which was formed in the sixteenth century or earlier. This one area, it appears, is excepted from the general law of theological development. One would like to know the basis of this exception; why authority in the Church, like liturgy, education, the press and communications, preaching and other activities of the Church, should not develop a theory and forms which are adapted to the twentieth-century man rather than to the sixteenth-century man. Obedience can change its forms and remain obedience; one who is a partner in a society rather than a subject can obey as a partner rather than as a subject. Authority need not be absolute in order to be true authority.

Possibly too much emphasis on an idea of authority formed in the absolutism of the sixteenth century may have obscured the vision of the original condition of authority in the Church as it is revealed in the New Testament. Theological treatment of authority has indeed employed texts of the New Testament, but the texts chosen dwell on certain aspects of authority rather than on the total idea, and on just those aspects which seemed to be under attack. Most theological treatises on authority have been more dependent upon the political theories of philosophers than upon the documents of the New Testament. The desire to make this area of theology harmonize with political theory is quite intelligible if the Church is conceived after the likeness of the State. If the Church is conceived in another way, political-ethical theory may be meaningless in interpreting the reality of the Church.

Part I. THE TEXTS
OF THE NEW TESTAMENT

1. The Head of the Church

OUR AREA OF INVESTIGATION is the idea of Church authority in the New Testament; and our first step is to study the texts in which the idea of authority and other ideas closely related to authority appear. I have tried to make this collection complete as far as the idea of authority directly is concerned; and this includes passages in which the use of authority in the apostolic Church is described. After the texts have been examined, we can attempt a synthesis.

The New Testament knows only one head of the Church, and that is Jesus Christ. To speak of Jesus Christ as the supreme authority in the Church would be such a ridiculous understatement that no one could think of using this designation; but authority in the Church has its reality and its intelligibility from its relationship to Jesus Christ. From this relationship authority enjoys whatever power of command it possesses, leaving room, as we have noticed, for legitimate development in the understanding and the use of authority. This relationship to Jesus Christ is the first and most fundamental factor which makes authority in the Church unlike any other authority.

There is no successor of Jesus Christ in the Church, nor could we think seriously of anyone carrying on his mission. The two realities on which this statement rests are of great importance in grasping the true nature of Church authority. First, Jesus Christ has never left the Church; he still lives in the Church and exercises his headship. Secondly, it is the whole Church in all its members which continues and extends the life and mission of Jesus Christ. The center of gravity in the Church is not the authority in the Church; if it were, the Church would be like other societies. The center of gravity is the enduring life of Christ in the Church which makes the Church the body of Christ. Authority in the Church exists within the body as all members exist within the body. The life of the Church flows from one head to all members, whether they be officers or others. Without the body and all its members the reality of the life and mission of Jesus Christ is not fulfilled; the life of the Church is not restricted to an elite group. These are basic theological truths which we shall encounter again in the treatment which follows. They should be borne in mind, for it is the life of the Church which gives rationality to authority in the Church. The life of the Church is the end which determines what authority, as a means, shall be.

The Church must be Christ, and she must know what Christ is. We cannot here cite all the Gospel texts which deal with the mission of Jesus, nor need we cite them; but we must look at those texts which touch the idea of authority directly or indirectly. The only Gospel passage in which Jesus summed up his ministry in a single sentence is found at the conclusion of a dispute concerning rank and place in the glory (or reign) of Jesus (Matthew 20:20–28; Mark 10:35–45; Luke 22–24–27 has preserved a part of the saying without either the incident of the request of the sons of Zebedee or the final sentence). The sons of Zebedee (in Matthew, their mother) asked for the two places next to Jesus in his glory. Jesus assured them a portion of his cup, but not the rank requested. The petition initiated a dispute which Jesus settled quickly. He contrasted the domination of secular rulers with the attitude which his followers should exhibit; the greatest in his group should be the *diakonos,* and the first in his group should be the slave. In this way they will be like him: "Just so the Son of Man did not come to receive service but to render service [*diakonein*] and to give his life as a ransom for many." I have left the Greek words *diakonos* and *diakonein* in the original for the moment; the usual translations, "minister" or "deacon," both of which have become ecclesiastical titles, obscure the force of the original. *Diakonos* means a lackey, a menial; when the abstract noun *diakonia* is translated into English by "service," the word suffers all the erosion which the English word has suffered. This is the term which Jesus uses to describe his own mission; and he insists that this is the proper term in which those of his followers whose position corresponds to the position of the great men of secular kingdoms should think of their own mission. In the New Testament, *diakonia* becomes almost a technical term for the apostolic ministry; and the term is traced back to Jesus himself. We shall encounter the term in our examination of the apostolic office, and we shall see that in the New Testament the words "lackey" and "slave" had not yet become "minister" and "servant." The same theme is clearly set forth in John 13:1–20, and the menial service of the washing of the feet is proposed by Jesus as an example of the service which the disciples should render each other.

This is a metaphor, and metaphors should not be pressed too hard. But the choice of one metaphor rather than another is significant. Jesus could have chosen other metaphors which would not have the same impact; he could, for instance, have compared the position of the Twelve to the position of the scribes in the Jewish community. As we shall see, he expressly rejected this comparison. The word *diakonia* and its cognates appear in profane Greek literature to designate other services than those of the lackey—much as the word "service" is used metaphorically in English—and the words are used in Greek of services rendered in religious groups. John 13:1–20 seems

to be written in answer to those who forget the original force
of the word. In the original force of the word, the *diakonos* is
a person whose function is not determined by his own will;
he is entirely at the disposal of others. Jesus not only washes
the feet of others, he puts his life at their disposal. Like all
metaphors, this metaphor breaks down, but it does not break
down with reference to the power of the *diakonos* over his
own acts or over the acts of others. It breaks down in the kind
of service the *diakonos* renders and in the identity of the
person to whose command he is submitted. The service of
Jesus is not determined by the arbitrary will of those whom
he serves as a slave, but by the will of the Father that the
diakonos should serve them by the complete surrender of
himself.

A discussion of the force of metaphors can easily degenerate
into logomachy. The metaphor is intended less as an exact
formula than as a means of creating a spirit and a sentiment.
No description of the spirit and the sentiment of the apostolic
community can be faithful unless it incorporates these words
of Jesus about the relation of himself to others as the model
of the relations of the members of the group to each other.
Whatever the metaphors of lackey and slave emphasize, it is
not power; and when "power" and similar words are used of
Jesus, it is necessary to examine them closely and see what
type of power is meant. This we shall do. In the passages
quoted above, the type of power exercised by secular rulers is
clearly excluded; to this we shall return. The spirit and the
sentiment created by this metaphor is not the spirit and the
sentiment of a community in which rulers and subjects are
sharply divided, but a community in which there is no emula-
tion except for the lowest position. The metaphor is a paradox
and a hyperbole, but one does not preserve the metaphor by
removing from it exactly those features which make it distinctive. Jesus himself refused to describe his own mission in

terms of rule over others; and the Church which carries on his mission must make his disclaimer her own. That this is not a total view of either the mission of Jesus or the mission of the Church is evident; no view which excludes these texts can be total either.

When power (*dynamis*) and authority (*exousia*) are given to Jesus in the Gospels, they are not of such a character as to nullify the conception of his mission as *diakonia*. The *dynamis* of Jesus is his power of miracles and, in particular, his power of exorcism. *Exousia* is attributed to his word (Matthew 7:29; Mark 1:22; Luke 4:32). *Exousia* in these passages signifies that Jesus has a commission to teach; the unspoken source of the commission is the Father, and Jesus as teacher is thus distinguished from the scribes who taught without a commission. The question of the priests and scribes about the authority of Jesus (Matthew 21:23; Mark 11:28; Luke 20:2) is also a question about the commission of Jesus; the unspoken source of the commission is again the Father, and this was the answer the priests and scribes expected. Instead of affirming his authority, Jesus refused to answer the question and proposed instead the dilemma of the commission of John the Baptist. The priests and scribes would not face the problem of the commission of John, and this was clear evidence that they would not face the problem of the commission of Jesus.

There is no parallel elsewhere in the Synoptic Gospels to the absolute authority which Jesus claims in Matthew 28:18. He does not transfer this authority to the disciples, for it cannot be transferred; but it is in virtue of this authority, given Jesus by the Father, that he commissions the Eleven to make disciples of all men, to baptize, and to teach the observance of all that he had commanded. Jesus fulfills the absolute scope of his own authority by a commission to the Eleven to make disciples everywhere. The commission to teach all that Jesus commanded must be treated when we come to the teaching

mission of the Church; we notice now that it is to be understood in the light of what the entire New Testament so often
calls the first, or the greatest, or even the only commandment.
The New Testament does not envisage the teaching of any
huge complex structure of obligations which would resemble
the Law as it was observed in Judaism of the New Testament
period.

These final verses of Matthew contain a theme which is
much more prominent in the Gospel of John. Whatever be the
reasons—whether disputes between early Christians and Jews
or disputes within the Christian community—there is a concern about the authority of Jesus in John which is not paralleled in the Synoptic Gospels. As samples of this concern, one
may read John 5:26–47 and 7:16–31. Here there are reiter-
ated denials that Jesus does or says anything of his own
authority; he speaks and acts by a commission which he has
received from the Father. The emphasis does not fall upon the
idea of power or upon the extent and scope of the power, but
on the fact that the authority of Jesus is received. The purpose
of these discourses is to present Jesus as the spokesman of the
Father whose commission is as genuine as the commission
of Moses. Because of the commission Jesus is empowered to
demand faith.

With this concern about the authority of Jesus there appears
in John the theme of *diakonia*. We have already noticed that
the episode of the washing of the feet is as graphic a presentation of the ideal of service as one could desire; and this episode
is connected with the supreme *diakonia* of Jesus—his death
on behalf of many. If one wishes another metaphor than the
metaphor of the slave and the lackey, he will find the mission
of Jesus described in John as the work of the shepherd (John
10:11–18). The figure could easily have been employed as an
image of the power to rule; "shepherd" was a conventional
royal title throughout the ancient Near East as well as in the

Old Testament, and without qualification royal power is what the figure would have suggested. But the figure is qualified; the determining feature of the good shepherd is that he lays down his life for his sheep. This is one of the few instances of the word *exousia*, which we have rendered "authority," in the Gospel of John. Jesus has received from the Father the authority to yield his life by his own free decision and not by exterior coercion or violence.

The other instances of *exousia* in John with reference to Jesus deserve a brief comment. Jesus is given authority to execute judgment (John 5:27). That Jesus is eschatological judge is a commonplace in the New Testament; but we are not considering here the eschatological manifestation of Jesus as lord and judge, since his eschatological functions can have no reference to the idea and use of authority in the Church. The Church continues his incarnational mission; he has not empowered the Church to anticipate his eschatological function, and in particular the New Testament is emphatic in its denial that his power of judgment is committed to anyone. The other instance of *exousia* (John 17:2) refers to the power over all flesh which Jesus has received from the Father; this is the power to confer eternal life. This power is obviously both incarnational and eschatological, and the Church shares in this power through its continuation of the incarnational mission. But in neither of these instances does *exousia* signify the power of domination or of jurisdiction; the authority of Jesus lies beyond these categories.

It has not been our purpose here to present a complete description of the mission of Jesus, if indeed such a complete description of his mission would be possible anywhere. We have tried to see how his own conception of his mission is related to authority. The texts which we have surveyed suggest that Jesus' own conception of his mission cannot be described as authoritarian. The feature which is emphasized is *diakonia*,

and that to such a degree that secular conceptions of authority
not only cannot be combined with his mission, but they are
explicitly excluded. Jesus does not dominate men, but invites
them to a free decision. If they refuse to make the decision,
they must accept the consequences; but he exercises no coercion upon them. The decision is motivated less by his words
than by his action of *diakonia*; it is action which he offers. He
has power from the Father, but it is presented as power to
serve and to save. To accept him is to accept him as the
diakonos of salvation. If his followers are to continue the mission which he has given them, they too must conceive of themselves as lackeys and slaves of others. This, we repeat, is not a
complete description of Church authority, but for our purpose
it is important to consider that only in these passages is the
mission of Jesus described with any relation to authority.

The sum of what we find concerning authority is certainly
general and indefinite enough; the Gospels are actually more
explicit concerning some false ideas of authority. Some of the
texts in which these ideas are mentioned we have noticed already; they should be studied more closely, for they contain
necessary correctives. Jesus was aware that the idea of authority in the community of disciples could easily be distorted
and thus lose its unique character. If this should happen, the
community itself would lose its identity and its purpose.

The story of the temptation of Jesus touches upon our problem. Only Matthew and Luke have the story of the three temptations, and the order of the three temptations differs in the two
Gospels. The offer of power over the kingdoms of the world is
placed third (and presumably in the climactic position) by
Matthew (4:8–10), second by Luke (4:5–9). Jesus rejects the
offer with a quotation from Deuteronomy 6:13 in which it is
commanded that worship be given to Yahweh alone. Certainly
the story means that secular power is not to be acquired at the
price of the worship of Satan; but do we grasp the import of

the story fully if we think that the only thing wrong with the offer of secular power is that it came from Satan? In the New Testament, "the world" in the pejorative sense is the realm of the power and the authority of Satan; the reign of God is opposed to this power, and the struggle between the two reigns is constant and deadly. St. Ignatius Loyola made this the theme of the meditation on Two Standards in the *Spiritual Exercises.* Like most Christian interpreters from early times, St. Ignatius did not question the implicit assertion in the temptation narrative that secular power is Satan's to give. The offer is not rejected because Satan is unable to deliver what he promises; it is rejected because secular power is altogether inept for the mission of Jesus, indeed because the use of secular power is hostile to his mission. The New Testament arose in the Roman world of the Caesar cult; in this world, the achieving of secular power through the grant of Satan made more sense than it does to us. Where the Caesar cult has vanished and nothing else has taken its place, we can conceive of secular power as something other than a grant of Satan; therefore we can conceive of it as something which can be integrated with the reign of God. Before we draw this conclusion too rapidly, there are other passages which we should consult. From the story of the temptation it is clear that "the power and glory of the kingdoms of this world" was rejected by Jesus, and we have to look carefully to see whether it is possible to modify secular power enough to make it acceptable in the reign of God.

Luke alone (12:13–14) has preserved a saying in which Jesus refuses a request to act as arbiter in a dispute of two brothers over their inheritance. The refusal is brusque; Jesus asks who has constituted him judge or arbiter. This was the type of problem which the scribes solve professionally; it is a legal problem with moral aspects. Yet Jesus will not touch it. He disclaims interest or competence in secular disputes. He will not take that position which the scribes occupied in the

Jewish community, because this position entitled the scribes to make personal decisions which belonged to others. The disputants were able to settle the dispute themselves. A solution imposed from outside would have been no solution. The anecdote is of particular interest because Jesus was here asked to exercise a type of authority which was common and recognized in the Jewish community. Although no one would have been surprised if he had accepted the request, we can conjecture that most observers were surprised that he refused it.

There are two stories of a dispute among the disciples about rank among themselves, and each dispute elicited a saying of Jesus. One of these we have already seen, and we must look at it again (Matthew 20:20–28; Mark 10:35–45; Luke 22:24–27). In an unusually close parallelism all three Gospels give the saying that the rulers of the nations dominate them, and the great among them exercise authority; Luke changes the second member to "those who exercise authority are called benefactors." "Benefactors" (*euergetēs*) was a royal title often taken by Hellenistic kings; the irony of Luke's variation is patent. In contrast to this, Jesus observes that it must not be so among the disciples; the great among them must be the lackey, and the first among them must be the slave. Another dispute is related in Matthew 18:1–5, Mark 9:33–37, and Luke 9:46–48. The saying of Jesus here has been connected by the catchword "child" in all three Gospels with the saying that the disciples should receive little children. But the point is clear. Jesus ends the dispute by telling the disciples that the greatest among them must be like a small child.

These two sayings are more than conventional exhortations to a vague humility. Children, lackeys, and slaves in ancient society were not the bearers of authority; indeed under most prevailing law they were not even persons. The saying of Jesus not only forbids self-assertion in general, but in particular that kind of self-assertion which is seen in the exercise of authority. Effectively his answer to the question of who is the greatest among the disciples is this: no one. He compares his group expressly with the authoritarian structure of existing civil society, and he prohibits the introduction of this authoritarian structure into the community of his disciples.

The Jewish community furnishes no model of authoritarian structure either. The discourse of Matthew 23 sums up most of the animadversions of Jesus upon Jewish leadership. He tells the disciples to do as the scribes and Pharisees say, but not as they do—which is as complete a condemnation of authority as has ever been compressed into a single sentence. They lay heavy obligations upon others which they themselves will not bear. They love vain display and the recognition of their authority. They are obstacles to those who wish to enter the reign of God. They are casuists who evade sacred obligations by verbal hairsplitting. They lay great stress on the trivial, and neglect the vital duties which involve persons. Worst of all—if anything is left—they are hypocrites.

If these sayings stood by themselves, they would be as clearly anti-authoritarian as anyone could wish. They do not stand alone, as we shall see, nor does the New Testament justify the conception of the Church as a horde without form and structure. But the sayings do make it clear that the structure is not to be modeled on the authority of the absolute State or on the religious leadership of Judaism. Jesus did not need to use words like "child," "lackey," and "slave" to describe the position of the leaders in his community; the vocabulary of both Greek and Aramaic is ample enough to permit a more restrained statement. If Jesus had wished to say that those in authority should rule with justice and kindness, there are a dozen ways in which this could have been said. But such words as "rule" are exactly the words which he did not use. The sayings reveal a new conception of society and of authority, which must be formed not on the model of secular government, but on the mission of Jesus himself.

Jesus intended to point out that the idea of secular power was as great a danger to the group as anything else; and the language in which he rejects this idea is so strong because strong language was needed. As we shall see, the apostolic commission and the apostolic office do not diminish the vigor of these sayings. These texts are basic in any scheme of the constitution of the Church. One can conceive of two dangers to the unity and the integrity of the Church: anarchy and the secularization of power. Of the two, Jesus spoke very little about the danger of anarchy; he spoke frequently and earnestly about the danger of the secularization of power. If the Church remains organized about her true center, which is Christian love infused by the indwelling Spirit, the Church can never collapse into anarchy. But if she turns into an authoritarian structure, Christian love is inhibited, and the authoritarian structure can itself become the occasion of anarchy.

One may say that if this interpretation is correct, then Jesus left no instructions on how the Church should be governed. I think this is a legitimate conclusion; he left instructions on how the Church is not to be governed, and that is according to the model of secular power. As long as this corrupting influence is excluded, he seemed to have little interest in how the leaders of the Church were to exercise their leadership. As we shall see, the apostolic Church exhibited a good deal of improvisation in its management. On the basis of what we have in the Gospels, it is difficult to see how the apostolic Church could have done anything else.

The conclusion to be drawn, if the above interpretation is correct, is not that Jesus left no instructions on how the Church should be governed, but that he commissioned the Church to find new forms and structure for an entirely new idea of human association—a community of love. In an organization capable of indefinite expansion in time and space, it is more vital that it have unity of spirit, achieved by the indwelling personal Spirit, than that it have rigid forms incapable of adaptation to cultural changes and the movement of history. The Church could not fulfil this commission unless Jesus also endowed it with the resources to find new forms. He did endow it with these resources in the ideal of *diakonia* in love, a new and revolutionary form of authority which Christians could see in his own personal life and mission. Apart from this, there is the incalculable resource of the Spirit dwelling in the members of the one body of Christ. These resources can be inhibited by the greatest danger pointed out by Jesus: the creeping secularization of authority. Lord Acton's saying that power tends to corrupt, and absolute power tends to corrupt absolutely, is no more than a paraphrase of these passages of the Gospels.

2. The Twelve and Peter

THERE IS A CONVENTIONAL PRINCIPLE of the interpretation of the Gospels which has long been in use, and it is of importance in the consideration of Church authority in the New Testament. The principle may be stated thus: one must distinguish between those sayings of Jesus which are addressed to the disciples as officers of the Church and those which are addressed to them as the whole Church. The principle implies a duality in the group of the disciples which presumably perseveres in the Church. It implies an inner group and an outer group. In modern terms, one may say it implies a distinction between active members and associate members.

The principle needs examination if for no other reason than that it implies a duality in the sayings of Jesus which cannot be found there. In form, the sayings of Jesus are addressed to the group which is present, called by various names of which one can distinguish only the Twelve as a distinct group. There is no doubt that the Twelve are a distinct group, and it is the purpose of this chapter to see what constituted the Twelve a distinct group. But "the Twelve" and "the disciples" are used interchangeably in the Gospels, and sayings are addressed to the Twelve which have as general an application as one can imagine. If we restrict certain sayings as uttered to the officers of the Church, we introduce a distinction which the Gospels do not make. All the sayings of Jesus are addressed to the whole Church, and some of them concern its officers. We have already noticed some such sayings. The point may seem trivial. I think it is not, for it is of some importance whether we think of the Church and its officers as a duality or of the Church with its officers as a unity. It is of importance whether we think of the mission of the Church as committed to the Church or to the officers of the Church. Let us follow the tone of the Gospels and study the passages which deal with the mission of the disciples as the mission of the Church. Subsequently we shall see how this mission was understood and executed in the apostolic Church.

The first disciples were called to be "fishers of men" (Matthew 4:19; Mark 1:17; Luke 5:10 has "hunter of men"). In Matthew and Mark the words are addressed to Peter and Andrew, to Peter alone in Luke; but in no case is it to be supposed that James and John, whose call occurs in the same context, are excluded from this designation. The phrase is an obvious metaphor for the proclamation of the gospel, and it is as valid for the whole Church as it is for the individual members addressed, for this kind of fishing and hunting is the work of the Church.

A discourse on the apostolic mission is reported in all three Synoptic Gospels, but with variations. As usual, Matthew's discourse is longer and more obviously arranged (Matthew 10:1–11:1). The parallels in Mark are found in two contexts (Mark 3:13–19 and 6:7–11). Luke also has the material in different contexts, but with a modification of his own: he relates the mission of the Twelve in 9:1–5, but Matthew's discourse to the Twelve is more closely paralleled in Luke's discourse to the seventy-two disciples (Luke 10:1–16); this discourse overlaps the discourse to the Twelve in a few passages. It appears that as early as Luke it seemed necessary to show that the missionary discourse was addressed to more than the core group of the Twelve.

In all three accounts the commission is described as power

over unclean spirits and diseases. But in all three, likewise, the emphasis in the discourse is on the proclamation of the gospel. The content of the gospel is described briefly as the arrival of the reign of God. Most of the discourse is concerned with how the missionaries are to conduct themselves and how they are to deal with those whom they address. There is a stern prohibition of any material resources: they are to travel without money or provisions and to live off the hospitality of those to whom they proclaim. If those whom they approach do not receive them, they are simply to abandon the unbelievers to the judgment of God.

Matthew 10:17–11 contains material which Luke has in scattered contexts or not at all. The topics treated are persecution, proclamation, and confession of Jesus without fear, divisions in families as a result of the gospel, and renunciation as a condition of discipleship. These topics are appropriate to the missionary discourse, but interpreters are agreed not only that the discourse is a composition of the type familiar in Matthew, but also that it is written in the light of the experiences of the early Church.

What is the relevance of this discourse to the question of Church authority? At first sight it appears to have no relevance, and this itself is relevant. The thrust in the apostolic Church was toward the proclamation of the gospel in the manner in which Jesus himself had proclaimed it; for it is the mission of Jesus which is described in the missionary discourse. The gospel is more than a message or a doctrine; it is a way of life, and it is on the way of life that the emphasis falls. The missionaries are to show in their deportment as well as in their proclamation that they carry on the war which Jesus initiated against worldly values. Is this addressed exclusively to the officers of the Church? Luke did not think so for those parts of the discourse which he placed in other contexts. The renunciation which Jesus imposes upon those who proclaim is elsewhere in the Gospels imposed upon all who wish to be his disciples. The missionary thrust appears also in the commission given in Matthew 28:18–20, already mentioned. The apostolic task is to make disciples of all nations, to baptize, and to teach the commandments of Jesus. And when the Eleven had to elect a replacement for Judas Iscariot, they defined membership in the Twelve as presence in the company from the baptism of John to the ascension of Jesus and bearing witness of the resurrection of Jesus.

We have not in these texts reached the idea of the Twelve as governing officers of the Church; but we have reached an idea of their office as the proclamation of the gospel, the witness of the resurrection, and the administration of baptism. This is the office in which authority must find its place; for Church authority is determined by the nature of the task which the Church has to perform. Its task is defined in the terms set forth above; and the Church has that authority which it needs in order to fulfil its ministry of the word and its ministry of the sacraments. There is no other basis for Church authority; and the space given to authority in the Gospels suggests that authority needs less attention than the apostolic mission proper, which must be fully understood. If the mission is understood, then the necessary forms of authority will develop.

The Twelve are promised thrones from which they will judge the twelve tribes of Israel (Matthew 19:28; Luke 22:30). This judgment in Matthew is clearly eschatological and almost certainly eschatological in Luke. As eschatological, it has no reference to the power and authority of the Twelve in the Church in the world. Very probably, by the Church is here meant the twelve tribes, for the Church is the fullness of the new Israel. One may see here an allusion to two other ideas. The one is the lordship which is given to Jesus in virtue of his passion and resurrection (*see,* for example, Romans

1:4). The Twelve, like Jesus, receive the fulfilment of their mission in the eschatological event. The second idea is the request of the sons of Zebedee for places of honor in the reign (Matthew 20:20–23; Mark 10:35–40). The request is left hanging in the air; the places of honor are assigned by the Father. Now Jesus announces that these places belong to the Twelve equally.

We observed that the Twelve have a distinct position in the Gospels. This position is more than constant and close association with Jesus. It is upon the Twelve primarily that the duty of the mission lies, the duty of proclamation, of witness, and of baptizing. In any definition of the apostolic office in New Testament terms these are the essential elements, and any other function is derived from the primary function. It is only in this connection that apostolic authority in the New Testament can be discussed; it is the mission which gives apostolic authority its genuine and unique character. How the apostolic Church regarded and exercised the apostolic office and apostolic authority we shall examine in the following chapter.

Peter has a special position in the Twelve, as the Twelve have a special position within the whole group of disciples. A review of the theological discussion of the primacy of Peter and its relationship to the primacy of the Roman Pontiff would take us far beyond the scope of a study of Church authority in the New Testament. Here, as in the entire question of authority, we intend to do no more than survey this element in its original form. The principle of the development of doctrine is applicable here with peculiar force; we have already noticed that no doctrine can be frozen in its new Testament form. On the other hand, we distort the New Testament if we attempt to find in it the term of the entire historical development of any doctrine, whether it be the primacy of the Roman Pontiff or the divine sonship of the Word. Such an approach is a denial of the development of doctrine.

The position of Peter, like the position of the Twelve, must be understood in the terms of the apostolic mission. It cannot be viewed abstractly as an isolated reality. The position of Peter is not only in the Church, it is for the Church; and the Church ultimately is the determinant of the position of Peter. This does not mean that the Church acts as a constitutional agent in deciding what the position of Peter shall be; Peter does not receive his position from the Church, nor does the Church receive its reality from Peter. It means simply that the reality of the Church and the position of Peter in the Church go together. We do not conceive of Jesus as establishing two things—a Church and its primate—but of establishing one thing, the Church in which is a primate. By establishing the Church, Jesus determined the position of Peter in the Church; for Peter is primate in the Church, not in something else, and it is the constitution of the Church which specifies his primacy.

That Peter is mentioned more frequently than the other disciples, that he speaks more than the others and sometimes speaks for them are matters of interest; but these facts do not establish his position among the Twelve. That Jesus changed his name from Simon to Peter does not establish his position. Even if we could show that Peter was a "natural leader" who assumed a kind of informal headship of the group under Jesus, this would not establish his position. Peter's position can be determined only by the commission which Jesus gave him and by the practice of the apostolic Church. All of the Gospels except Mark contain some kind of commission given to Peter: and there is no ambiguity about Peter's leadership of the Jerusalem community in the book of Acts.

While all three Synoptic Gospels contain the episode of the confession of Peter (Matthew 16:13–20; Mark 8:27–30; Luke

9:18–21), only Matthew has the lines in which Peter is called
the rock on which the Church is built, and is promised the keys
of the reign and the power of binding and loosing. Here Peter
is the spokesman of the group on a solemn occasion, for he
confesses his belief that Jesus is the Messiah. The text of
Matthew does suggest that the commission is given to Peter
in return for his profession of faith. To this we shall return.

The absence of the lines in Mark and Luke is an ancient
exegetical problem, and the solution frequently proposed is
that Mark and Luke lack the lines because Jesus did not utter
them. A solution adopted in apologetic theology is that Mark
omits the lines because of the modesty of Peter, the presumed
source of Mark, and that Luke omitted them because their
equivalent is found in Luke 22:31–32. Neither of these solutions carries much conviction. Oscar Cullmann has suggested
that Mark and Luke lack the lines because they were not
uttered in this context, and a number of interpreters think
that the lines belong to the post-resurrection words of Jesus.
The conclusion that Mark and Luke do not have the lines because they did not know them seems inescapable, and the
source of the lines in Matthew is no more of a problem than
the source of other lines peculiar to Matthew or to Luke. The
question is not solved by affirming or denying that the lines
contain "the very words" of Jesus. The apostolic Church could
and did form the sayings of Jesus in its own way, as we know
from a study of the parallels in the Synoptic Gospels. Matthew
contains one expression of the belief of the apostolic Church
that Jesus had given Peter a position which Peter did not share
with the other members of the Twelve. We shall meet this belief in other texts.

What was this position? The emphatic tone and the deceptive clarity of the text of Matthew have led some theologians
to treat the passage as if it stood alone with no other witness
to the position of Peter. It has been thought to say all there is

to be said and to need no explanation or supplement from other texts. We have alluded to the dangers of metaphor in the Bible; here we have a set of metaphors which have been taken as seriously as figures of speech can be taken. One has to marvel at the reasoning by which a rock and keys become full-fledged jurisdictional power defined in purely political terms. One can understand the anxiety of nineteenth-century theologians to found pontifical authority securely in the New Testament; we have noticed that authority was on the defensive. One can understand the exegetical pressure applied to the text of Matthew, for, as we have seen and shall see again, the number of New Testament texts which deal directly with a commission of authority is remarkably small. But we are now able to locate these texts in the context of the mission of Christ and the Church. This understanding, I believe, far from minimizing the texts (a bad word in contemporary theology) will reveal a richness of meaning which has not been exploited in recent theology.

The rock is a common Old Testament metaphor, but not as the foundation upon which a house is built. This obvious metaphor, however, appears in Matthew 7:24 and Luke 6:48 where the rock on which the house (not the Church) is built is the words of Jesus. In the Old Testament the rock is a secure defensive position from which one can repel attack. In this sense, Yahweh himself is called a "rock" or even addressed as "rock." The word "rock," which by a word play becomes the personal name of Peter (Aramaic, *kē' pa'*; Greek, *petra*) evokes all these Old Testament associations.

The meaning of Peter as the rock upon which the Church is built must be understood in terms of the Church which is built upon the rock. The Church appears in the Gospels as a group which has the mission of proclaiming the gospel and of baptizing. To call Peter the rock upon which this group rests is to give him more than mere leadership or mere jurisdictional power. Here the connection between the confession of Peter and the title of rock becomes apparent. The group proclaims that which it believes; Peter, who by the revelation of the Father has had an insight into the Messiahship of Jesus, exhibits the kind of faith on which the group can rest securely. The rock upon which the Church rests is the faith of Peter not understood as a merely personal act, but as embodying the faith upon which the Church depends for the fulfilment of her mission. The same idea occurs in Luke 22:31–32 to which we shall refer below.

Were this all that was said, the text would present Peter as no more than a leader in faith, an interpretation which was favored by the majority of earlier Protestant theologians. But this is not all. The metaphor of the keys is the clearest figure of authority which we have yet encountered. In Isaiah 22:22, Eliakim receives the keys of the royal palace of Jerusalem. Eliakim held the office of "the one over the house," or master of the palace, one of the highest ranking offices in ancient Near Eastern monarchies; and the key was the symbol of the office. Jesus could not have said more clearly that Peter becomes master of the palace in the Church. If the term is carried further, it means that Peter has the management of the domestic affairs of the Church; but here we run the danger of pressing the metaphor too closely. We must define Peter's office in the terms of the Church and its mission of proclamation and baptizing. To specify beyond this is to do something which the gospel does not do; the form of management is left open to development.

The metaphor of binding and loosing is obscure; it has no antecedents in biblical language. It seems doubtful that the phrase is used in the sense found in the rabbinical writings, where "bind" signifies a decision imposing an obligation, and "loose" a decision releasing from an obligation. Nothing in this particular context or in the New Testament idea of the apostolic office indicates that the office is to be considered rabbinical in character. On the other hand, Matthew has a number of allusions to Jewish practices which are not found in the other Gospels. The phrase certainly signifies a power of decision. The two words are applied to the entire group in Matthew 18:18 which we shall discuss subsequently.

The faith of Peter is associated with a commission to Peter in Luke 22:31–32 mentioned above. Like the text of Matthew, these lines of Luke are not paralleled in the other Gospels. Jesus tells Peter that he has prayed for Peter that his faith should not fail and that, after his conversion, Peter should "confirm" his brethren. Interpreters see here an allusion to the denial of Peter; and it is from this lapse of faith that he is converted. The word "confirm" may contain an interesting word play. The Greek word used is *stērizein*, to make hard or firm. The assonant Greek word *stereōma* is one of the words used in the Greek Old Testament to render the Hebrew *selao*, rock. Whether the word play is intentional or not, the work of Peter is to communicate to his brethren that firmness of faith from which he got his name. As in Matthew, the special position of Peter is, in the first place, leadership in faith.

John 21:15–19 contains yet another statement of the special position of Peter. This passage also echoes the denial of Peter; for he is asked for a triple profession of love. In response to his profession Peter is given the commission to act as shepherd of the flock of Jesus. Here, as in the metaphor of the keys, there is a clear and unambiguous term which indicates authority. We have already noticed that the title of "shepherd" is a common designation of kings in the Old Testament and in the ancient Near East; it appears in the Homeric poems also. Part of the royal insignia of the Egyptian king was the shepherd's crook. But Jesus himself is the shepherd of his flock, as we have seen, and, in calling Peter, the shepherd Jesus neither renounces his own position nor does he make

Peter a type of shepherd different from himself. Peter also must be the good shepherd, whose dedication is tested by his readiness to die for his sheep. The figure of the good shepherd indeed indicates authority, but even more emphatically it evokes the image of the good shepherd, whose mission is to save. The verses which follow are a prediction that Peter will die for his responsibility; this is the supreme *diakonia*, the true work of the shepherd who is entrusted with the flock of Jesus. The commission does indicate responsibility, and it shows the type of responsibility which Jesus lays upon the leaders of his community. Like him, they are to serve, not to be served.

The commission given to Peter in John is not based on faith, but on love of Jesus. Peter stoutly refuses to assert that he loves Jesus more than any other of the disciples love him; this is not required for his commission. But the love which is the action of faith is required. There is some artistry in the fact that the question whether Peter loves more than the others is dropped after the first interrogation. Peter is to prove his profession of love by feeding the flock. If his love of Jesus is genuine, he will direct it to those of whom he has the care as shepherd. His love of them will be the medium through which they experience the love of Jesus the shepherd. We have a term which indicates authority, but we are somewhat remote from ideas of domination.

These texts give us the ideas of master of the palace and shepherd; they give us the idea of leadership in faith and the active love of one whose first care is the flock for which Jesus died and for whom the shepherd must be ready to die. Having this, we have a great deal. This is Christian leadership of a Christian community, leadership which mediates the active presence of Christ manifesting and executing his own mission. It is leadership which is wholly identified with the Church and with its members and its mission. The dominant ideas in the passages are faith and love, and no particular details of rule and government are even hinted. If Peter shows leadership in faith and love, the demands of the Church are satisfied.

That Peter acts as the leader of the Jerusalem community in Acts 1–12 needs no demonstration and is not disputed. He is the spokesman of the group, whether in its own meetings, in the proclamation of the gospel, or in defense of the group before the Jewish council. He initiates the election of Matthias, acts for the Twelve in the collection of goods renounced by the members, begins the mission to the Gentiles, and justifies the mission before the rest of the apostolic group. His leadership in Acts 1–12 is as evident as his almost total disappearance from the book after these chapters is puzzling. He appears after Acts 12 only as one of the speakers at the council held in Acts 15, and here he speaks with others in favor of the decision which was finally adopted by the group. Paul (Galatians 1:18–2:14) recognizes him with James and John as one of the "pillars" of the Jerusalem church and, indeed, as a very influential man whose compromise with the Judaizing faction was damaging. We owe to Paul also (Galatians 2:7–8) the information that Peter had a mission to Jews outside Palestine corresponding to Paul's mission to Gentiles. There is some uncertainty in the details of this period, but we have a picture of Peter as a leader of the apostolic Church.

Peter, however, does not appear clearly as *the* leader of the apostolic Church, and this causes some anguish. There is an unspoken apprehension that if Peter does not appear as the leader in a manner at least substantially resembling the leadership of the Roman Pontiff in centuries much later, there is something wrong either with Peter or with the Roman pontiffs. As I have pointed out, perhaps so often that it has become tedious, the principle of the development of doctrine makes this apprehension unnecessary. We have seen that the terms of Peter's commission are left quite general. How Peter implemented the terms is not imposed as a model in all details for

other times and places; we study his commission in order to
see what is basic in it.

In the first place, we must notice that no one else appears
in a position of leadership corresponding to the leadership of
Peter. If any competitor is alleged, it would have to be James.
However, we do not know enough about James to make
definite assertions, and we have nothing at all for James which
corresponds to the Gospel texts concerning the commission
of Peter. Paul does not conduct himself as the head of the
Church, as we shall see; but he creates something of a problem by recognizing no one else as head. Paul was careful with
the Jerusalem church with which he wished to remain on good
terms. He wished to leave no doubt that his gospel was identical with the gospel preached by the Church as a whole; but
he recognized obedience to no central headquarters. Once he
received his commission from the church of Antioch (Acts
13:1–3), he acted independently, not even professing submission to the church of Antioch. His call to be an apostle came
from Jesus Christ, not from the church of Antioch. His claim
was that he was an apostle as much as anyone else who bore
the title; nothing further, it seems, was required.

Plainly, then, Peter's leadership was anything but absolute.
We have no clear instance of a decision which he made without associating himself with other members of the group. Even
in Acts 1–12, where his leadership is best seen, decisions are
made by "The Twelve," or "the apostles," or "the church,"
and not by Peter. His action in Acts 10 was reviewed by "the
party of the circumcision" (Acts 11:1–18). His devious be-
havior at Antioch was openly rebuked by Paul (Galatians
2:11–14). In fact, Peter's relationship to the officers of the
Jerusalem church is best designated by a term which has become common in recent theological discussion: collegiality.
The type of leadership exercised by Peter in Acts 1–12 corresponds exactly to the type of leadership sketched in the

Gospel texts we have cited. And this is not surprising, for the book of Acts and the Gospels are the voices of the same apostolic Church. The leadership of Peter was entirely compatible with decisions reached by the common consent of a group.

For this reason the term "leadership" describes Peter's position better than the term "government." We shall see that this simple structure of the apostolic Church did not endure even through the apostolic age; but this simple structure is not out of harmony with the constitution of the Church and the commission which Jesus gave to the Twelve and to Peter. It is leadership determined by the mission of the Church and, therefore, not self-conscious about itself. It is responsibility simply accepted and simply met; it is *diakonia* in action. We shall see that this ideal, so well embodied in Peter, appears with equal clarity in other areas of Church authority in the New Testament.

3. The Apostolic Office

"THE TWELVE" AND "THE APOSTLES" are not perfectly identical groups in the New Testament. Paul was an apostle, but he was not one of the Twelve. By combining material from various texts (which we need not set forth here), scholars conclude that an apostle was one who had seen the risen Jesus and who had a personal commission from Jesus to proclaim the gospel. The number who could claim the title is not determined, but that the title was important is clear from Paul's insistence on his right to be called an apostle. If there are any officers of the Church in the New Testament, they are apostles; and for our study the apostolate is of the first importance.

The Greek word, *apostolos*, from which our English word "apostle" comes, means in classical Greek literature a naval expedition and, in later literature, a delegate or a messenger. There is no parallel in Greek to the religious use of the word; but in Judaism the corresponding Aramaic word was a title given to men sent from Jerusalem to Jewish communities abroad. This may have influenced the Christian use of the word.

We saw in considering the position of Peter that he exercised his leadership in association with the group of apostles. The first action, as we should expect, was the proclamation of the gospel by Peter and the other apostles. Peter spoke for all when he affirmed before the Jewish council the right and the duty of the apostles to proclaim the gospel (Acts 4:5–21 and

5:27–42). The duty of proclamation is again affirmed when the apostles ask for the selection of six or seven men who will free them from the duty of distributing food in order that their ministry of the word may be unimpeded (Acts 6:1–4). For the only act of "management" which we find in the Jerusalem church had to do with the acceptance and the administration of the goods renounced by those who joined the community (Acts 4:32–35). In the communism of the primitive Church each member turned over his possessions to a common pool from which the apostles distributed to each according to need. Luke draws an ideal picture of a community of one heart and one soul (Acts 4:32), and obviously in such a community the management was rather loose; but no church is any more ideally the Church because it is not of one heart and one soul and substitutes enforcement for unity of sentiment and purpose. That there were delinquents in the Jerusalem church is seen in the story of Ananias and Sapphira (Acts 5:1–11), and it may be regarded as fortunate that the consequences of apostolic admonition which are related in this popular anecdote are not typical of ecclesiastical administration everywhere. Ananias and his wife had sinned against the Holy Spirit, the principle of unity of the Church.

Other decisions are made by the apostles. They send Peter and John to those whom Philip had baptized at Samaria (Acts 8:14) and Barnabas to Antioch (Acts 11:22). The church of Antioch, in turn, dispatched Barnabas and Saul on their mission to the Gentiles (Acts 13:1–3). The church of Jerusalem examined and finally ratified Peter's baptism of Gentiles (Acts 11:1–18). When the major problem arose of the standing of Gentiles in the Church and the degree to which Jewish observance should be obligatory for the Gentiles, Luke relates that this problem was settled by a council of the apostles and elders of the church of Jerusalem (Acts 15). Because Paul does not mention this assembly, a number of recent interpreters think that Luke has telescoped a number of discussions into an assembly which never met as Luke describes it; but this does not affect our consideration of the exercise of the apostolic office. Luke did not think he described something foreign to the practice of the Church when he described an assembly which reached a decision by common consent after full deliberation. The apostolic office, like the leadership of Peter, was not exercised in an absolute manner. However, the decision, when it was reached, was an authoritative decision; it was presented with the force which the situation required. We see apostolic authority evolving as the Church grows and problems multiply. A Church which had reached deeply into Europe from Palestine was no longer a group "of one heart and one soul" in the sense that everyone knew everyone else and all shared a common cultural heritage. And it is not without interest that the first such sweeping act of apostolic authority recorded in the New Testament is a release from obligations.

This is also the last such act which the New Testament records. The primitive Church lost its center when Jerusalem was destroyed by the Romans in 70 A.D. The Palestinian church seems to have perished in this disaster, and, when another center appeared, it came after New Testament times and therefore lies outside the scope of this study. For further information on the apostolic office we turn to the most ample source on the subject: the epistles of Paul.

We owe Paul's treatment of the apostolic office to the fact that his mission was questioned at Corinth; and it should be remembered that Paul's writing in 1–2 Corinthians about the apostolic office is defensive. This does not mean that his idea is distorted, but that the polemic intent of his treatment is responsible for the tone and emphasis of the epistles. Paul asserts his authority because it was questioned; we do not find similar assertions in the other letters written to churches which did not question his apostolic mission. The defensive purpose of Paul's letters to the Corinthians has made his treatment rhetorical rather than theological; he writes with passion and not with cold reason.

Employing, on the passages of 1 Corinthians where Paul treats of the apostolic office, some of that cold reason which he did not use, we see that the apostle is a bringer of all spiritual gifts (1:7), the herald of Christ crucified (1:23 and 2:2) in the Spirit and power (2:4). The apostle plants what God brings to maturity (3:6). He is God's fellow worker (3:9), the builder of the Church on the foundation of Jesus Christ (3:10–11), the servant of Christ and the steward of God's mysteries (4:1), the father of the Church in Christ through the gospel (4:15). The apostle is under the necessity of proclaiming the gospel, and he does no more than he ought when he proclaims it (9:16). He is the slave of all who becomes all things to all men (9:19–22).

The apostle, we have noticed, is one who has seen the risen Jesus (1 Corinthians 9:1) and who has received a personal commission from Jesus to proclaim the gospel (Galatians 1:11–16; 1 Corinthians 15:8–10). But the mark of the genuine apostle in Paul's rhetoric is his suffering for the gospel. In a passage written with irony, Paul calls the apostles men condemned to death, a spectacle to angels and to men, fools, weak, disreputable, needy, reviled and persecuted, the refuse of the world (1 Corinthians 4:9–13). The apostle becomes all these things in his proclamation of the gospel. In 2 Corinthians 11:23–28, Paul recites the misadventures which have befallen him in his missions—flogging, imprisonment, shipwreck, fatigue, enmity everywhere—and, to top it all, the daily pressure of the responsibility of his churches. The apostle who has not known the pains of missionary work, Paul would say, has not engaged in missionary work. The apostle is recognized as genuine because he bears on his body the marks of Jesus (Galatians 6:17).

The exercise of apostolic authority was developed with the

rise of problems in the churches, and Paul's epistles, particularly 1 Corinthians, illustrate the development. Paul had the disagreeable duty of pronouncing judgment on those who were delinquent (1 Corinthians 5:1–13). That he found this duty painful is apparent from 2 Corinthians 1:23–2:11, in which he admits the offenders to reconciliation. Paul's judgment did not have the sensational consequences of which we read in the story of Ananias and Sapphira; his punishment was expulsion from the Christian community—the early form of excommunication. It is doubtful that any more than expulsion is meant by the deliverance of the offender to Satan for the destruction of the flesh (1 Corinthians 5:5); and it should be noticed that Paul's sentence was medicinal, not vindictive; his purpose was the salvation of the spirit of the offender.

If we knew more about the factions of the church of Corinth, we should be better able to understand why Paul seems rather restrained in his appeal for unity and harmony (1 Corinthians 1:10–3:23). It seems unlikely that the factions could have seriously threatened Christian love or unity of doctrine in the Corinthian community. When Paul's gospel was attacked by the Judaizers who wished to impose the observance of the Law as a condition of salvation, Paul spoke with much more vigor (Galatians 1:6–10 and 3:1–5). But Paul knew that love and unity cannot be imposed by authority; they must arise from the free personal decision of each member of the community. It is a free personal decision to which Paul appeals, employing all the motives which the gospel presents for this unity. Paul did not solve all problems by a single technique.

The infant churches had questions for which there was no explicit answer in the proclamation and certainly not in precedent; and 1 Corinthians is written mostly in answer to such questions. When Paul deals with these problems, he is generally decisive and authoritative, but one notices again that his tactics vary with the type of problem presented. He has no doubt that it is simply unchristian for members of the church to take their differences before civil courts (1 Corinthians 6:1–8); Christian love is a principle which should resolve any dispute. Paul writes at greater length on the problems of marriage and virginity (1 Corinthians 7), distinguishing the teaching of the Lord from his own recommendations, and founding both in theological argument. He does not impose his solutions by pure decree, but he does what he can to make them reasonable. Similarly, he explains his answer to the question of eating meat which has been sacrificed to idols and the problem of scandal created by this practice (1 Corinthians 8). These questions sometimes lead him into little essays or homilies on the general principles of Christian belief and Christian life, disquisitions which go beyond the immediate problem but are the most precious parts of the epistles. They show his unceasing effort to place his answer or his precept in a context in which they are intelligible and acceptable. Evidently he wished the Corinthians to understand why their belief and their practice took the form which he gave it in his teaching. His weakest argument, certainly, is the argument which supports the covering of women's heads at worship (1 Corinthians 11:1–16). Like most disputants, Paul is prolix where his arguments are less convincing, and this is the point where Paul ultimately falls back on what has since become a venerable argument in ecclesiastical discipline: "This is the way we have always done it." Paul is intolerant of abuses in the Eucharistic rite (1 Corinthians 11:17–33). The problem of the charismata is discussed at greater length than any other (1 Corinthians 12–14), and before Paul has finished with this problem (which seems somewhat unreal to us), he has written essays on the Church as the body of Christ and on the perfection of love, the supreme charisma (1 Corinthians 12:12–14:1).

Paul even engaged in fund-raising. The desperate need of

the Palestinian community due to a famine was met by col-
lections in Paul's churches. His interest in this project is evident from 1 Corinthians 16:1–4 and 2 Corinthians 8–9. The
motives for contribution to the needs of others have never
been set forth so clearly or with such a deep foundation in
Christian morality. The tone of Paul's appeal to the Corinthians is so much at variance with the context in which Paul
admonishes them severely that most critics believe 2 Corinthians, as it stands, is not a single letter, but a collection of
passages from different letters. This opinion is highly probable;
at the same time, we should not underestimate Paul's capacity
to turn suddenly from admonition (and that in sharp tones)
to a delicate appeal for generosity to the point where the resources of all are equalized.

Here we have a picture of apostolic authority at work in
the management of the churches. Paul recognizes the primary
apostolic duty of proclaiming the gospel. He knows that the
apostle must share in the passion of Jesus if his proclamation
is to bear fruit. But once the Christian communities were established, more than proclamation was demanded. The apostle
must answer questions clearly and decisively. He must make
ordinances not only for the procedure in such strictly ecclesiastical matters as worship, but also for the conduct of Christians in their relations with the world. He must instruct more
fully in the content of the gospel and he must show the relevance of the gospel to the daily life of the believer. He must
admonish and correct when it is necessary, and he must use
the supreme punishment of exclusion if he has to; but when
he uses his power to punish, he has in view the recovery of the
delinquent whom he must punish. Having said all this, we sum
up the functions which we see in 1 Corinthians, and which
could be illustrated as well from most of the other epistles. But
having said this, we still have not caught the heart and soul
of the apostolic office as Paul exercised it. Perhaps we cannot
catch them, but the effort should be made.

We may notice, first, that Paul does not exercise his apostolic authority in an absolute manner, just as we have seen for Peter and the Twelve. Paul was criticized by some of the Corinthians harshly and unjustly. He responded to the criticisms with warmth, but he did not affirm that he was above criticism. He read the incestuous man out of the Church, but he did not read his own critics out of the Church. In 1–2 Corinthians and Galatians he conducts a kind of running debate with his refractory Christians. He is firm and unyielding where he must be, ready to compromise where he can; but he has a conversation with them, not a lecture. He listens to them and answers them because he evidently regarded that victory which is achieved by sheer weight and not by persuasion and conviction as no victory at all. In Paul's mind the members of the churches shared in the apostolic office and the apostolic responsibility, and he thought that they were entitled to know why he told them what he did and to have their questions and objections answered.

We can see in the epistles why an absolute exercise of authority did not occur to Paul and could not. The churches of Corinth, Galatia, Philippi and Thessalonica were his own churches in a personal way. Another man could not refer to the labors and pains these churches had cost him, and still retain his personal dignity. The least of Paul's concerns was his personal dignity. Paul's dealings with these churches were intimate and unconstrained; his epistles are not the communications of a superior to subjects or of an administrator to subordinates so much as an unabashed disclosure of the heart to close friends. We do not know how Paul achieved this level of interpersonal communication with his Christians. Obviously they did not look upon him as the modern Catholic looks upon his bishop. Paul belonged to his Christians, and they belonged to him; and this is the way they treated each other. The relation of apostle and Christians which he established is unique; it is not like the relations of members of a family or of a civil

society. Paul did what we said Jesus committed to the Church
to do: he brought into being an entirely new and original idea
of authority. The words *diakonos* and *diakonia*, which we
noticed in the Gospels as designations of the mission of Jesus,
occur more frequently in the Pauline writings to designate the
apostle and the apostolic office than they do in the rest of the
entire New Testament. When we study the man and his work,
we see how Paul translated this ideal into reality.

To put this new and original idea on a solid basis, we can
suggest that Paul's dedication was not to a message, or an idea,
or an institution; he was dedicated to persons—the persons to
whom he proclaimed the gospel and whom he admitted to the
Church. His personal dedication to Jesus Christ is transparent
on every page of the epistles, but he did not conceive his
dedication to Jesus Christ as something detached from his
dedication to his Christians. In them and only in them could
he find a real Christ to love and serve; for they are the body
of the Christ who lived in Paul and in whom Paul lived. Authority for Paul was a function of love, a personal love directed
to individuals whom he could name; it was not an organizational function. Authority had no end and purpose other than
the persons for whom Paul was responsible and whom he
served to the point of annihilation of self. In this practical way
Paul knew that Christ is in the Church and in each member
of the Church, that if one seeks Christ, one will not find him
by looking outside of people. Authority is *diakonia* only if it
is service given to real existing persons.

4. The Spirit of Christ in the Body of Christ

THE CHURCH, IN THE LUCAN CONCEPTION, comes into being with the descent of the Spirit of Pentecost (Acts 2). The transforming effect of the Spirit is at once apparent. The disciples, previously timid and ineffective, are filled with speech and power and at once begin to proclaim the gospel with marvelous success. Luke attributes to the proclamation of the apostles in Acts effects far beyond any related of the proclamation of Jesus; the number of those who believe the proclamation of the apostles runs into the thousands. The Spirit dominates Acts 1–12, the account of the growth of the apostolic Church from the original group of disciples (counted by Luke at 120, Acts 1:15). The Spirit is a vital element in the authority of the Church. We have noticed more than once that the Church has the task of creating a new idea and a new use of authority; the Spirit is the agent who executes the new idea. We observe here, as we have observed before, that the primary element in the apostolic office—the work of proclamation—is the point where the operation of the Spirit is first manifested.

The conception of Luke is entirely in harmony with the conception of John. In John's conception, the Spirit is not given until Jesus is glorified (John 7:39). When the Spirit comes, it will be an "advocate" (John 14:16,26); it will teach the disciples all things (14:26); it will bear witness to Jesus (15:26); it will guide the disciples to all truth (16:13). Here, too, it is the Spirit through whom the Apostles will fulfill the mission of proclamation. The Synoptic Gospels too, although more rarely, attest the belief that the Spirit will empower the disciples to bear witness to Jesus (Matthew 10:19–20; Luke 12:11–12).

The Spirit is given to the whole Church and not exclusively to the leaders of the Church. At baptism the believers receive the Spirit through the imposition of hands (Acts 8:15–18 and 19:1–7) or without it (Acts 10:44). The coming of the Spirit was attested in a sensible manner by the gifts which are called *charismata*, in particular the gift of prophecy and the gift of tongues. The manifestation of these gifts was a sure sign that the Spirit had come and, therefore, that faith was genuine. When Gentiles were baptized, the doubt about their admission was resolved by the *charismata* which proved that the Spirit had come to them (Acts 10:44–48; 15:8–9). We have noticed that the reception of the *charismata* at Corinth became a routine event which needed regular direction. Here is suggested the position of the apostolic college in relation to the Spirit and to the entire membership of the Church, a position which is maintained in the hierarchical body which succeeds the apostolic college. The Spirit dwells in the entire Church, but is centered in the college. In a proper sense the Spirit is mediated to the rest of the Church from the college through the offices of the proclamation of the gospel and the administration of the sacraments. But the college must mediate the Spirit in other ways besides these, and the primary way is through personal influence, that is, through the love which is identified with the indwelling Spirit.

The idea of the Church as a single body inspired by a single Spirit is fundamental for the consideration of authority in the Church; and we must look more closely at the texts of Paul in which this idea is set forth. There are two passages, somewhat similar in content, where Paul speaks of the Spirit in the whole Church: 1 Corinthians 12:1–28 was written earlier than Romans 12:3–8. Furthermore, 1 Corinthians was written to a church which Paul knew personally and which presented disciplinary problems in its *charismata*; the fuller exposition of 1 Corinthians 12–14 is summed up briefly in Romans with no particular applications, since Paul had never been to Rome and knew the Roman church only by hearsay. But the principle of the Spirit animating the whole Church and all its members is not modified from the first letter to the later letter.

The weight of 1 Corinthians 12 falls upon the theme that the Church is one and the Spirit is one in spite of the diversity of functions and offices; Paul is concerned not with the diversity of the Church, but with its unity. He is also aware that diversity can become disintegration precisely in the area of offices and functions. God has given various gifts: the speech of wisdom or of knowledge, the gift of faith, miracles, prophecy, the discernment of spirits, and the interpretation of tongues. But these are diverse operations of one and the same Spirit. All these gifts and their possessors are related to each other as members of the body with different functions. The members need each other; it is in the life of the whole body that the diverse functions have meaning and value. Paul concludes his treatise with a reference to the offices of apostle, prophet, and teacher to which he adds in the same enumeration miracles, healers, helpers, administrators, and speakers of tongues. No one has every office, but all have the Spirit which inspires all offices. Paul then turns to the supreme *charisma*, the gift of love. This gift is the climactic operation of the Spirit, the work which is most truly the work of the Church and the fulfilment of the mission of Jesus, the *charisma* which alone gives meaning and value to all the *charismata* previously enumerated. In a church which is not a community of love, the Spirit is not present, and any *charismata* which may appear are certainly spurious.

The emphasis in Romans 12:3–8 is less on unity of Spirit and diversity of functions than on the acceptance by each member of the Church of the function which is his and, by implication, of the functions which belong to others. Each member has a *charisma* which he should use: prophecy, *diakonia*, exhorting, teaching, contributing, helping, doing acts of mercy; Paul here stresses those functions which can be summed up as "works of charity." He uses again the analogy of the body in which the members are interdependent. In a healthy body all the members perform their functions properly; atrophy of members is not a sign of good health.

I have said that the idea of the one Spirit in the one body is fundamental for the idea of authority in the Church. In common thought and language authority means power. In the Church the power of authority is identified with the Spirit. The operation of the Spirit is manifest in authority as it is manifest in all the operations of the Church performed by any of its members. The power which authority has is the same power which each member of the Church possesses; the power is manifested in different works. Paul states that no one can even profess that Jesus is Lord except in the Spirit (1 Corinthians 12:3). Authority exercised through any other species of power is not Church authority. That authority is one of the works of the Spirit demands that authority be respected as such; that other works of the Church are also works of the Spirit demands that the bearers of authority respect the other works as such.

If one wishes to define the power of the Spirit more closely, whether in authority or in other operations, one comes to Paul's statement that the supreme *charisma* is love. This will specify authority as it specifies all works of the Spirit. We recall what was said in the preceding chapter concerning the

idea and use of authority which can be gathered from the
epistles of Paul; and we see in him the exemplar of what authority, as a function of love, can be. The works of authority
in the Church are determined by the mission of the Church.
Authority is instituted to exercise leadership in the ministry
of the word and in the ministry of the sacraments. This commission carries with it the power to make all dispositions in
the Church which are necessary to the fulfilment of the mission. The base of the power of authority is the love which
those in authority exhibit; for the mission of the Church is
the work of the love of Jesus Christ for men. Authority is a
commission to lead in love and in the service of love; this, and
not a grant of dominative or jurisdictional power in the secular
sense, is what enables authority to exercise its leadership and
to demand the assent of the other members of the Church.
This conception of authority, far from diminishing its scope,
increases it; for all men know that love can demand and obtain
a response far in excess of the response which can be demanded by mere dominative and jurisdictional power. These
types of power are not only poor substitutes for love in the
Church; they are not substitutes at all.

I have said that the base of power is the love which authority exhibits, and not the love which it claims. Love is the
supreme work of the Spirit both in authority and in those
under authority. Where either fails in love, Church authority
breaks down. But neither those who have authority nor those
under authority are dispensed from the work of love because
the object of love fails in its duty of love. Neither the one nor
the other shows love by supporting the other precisely in its
failure to love. The first duty both of authority and of those
under authority is to foster love, and each fosters love best by
performing the works of love. In a community of love, such
as the Church, good discipline and obedience to duly constituted authority are not necessarily signs of the operation of

the Spirit. These effects can be achieved in a well regulated army or prison. If authority seeks no more than discipline and obedience, it does not seek the works of the Spirit.

Adolph Harnack once introduced a distinction between charismatic offices and hierarchical offices in the early Church. In this view, the close relation between Spirit and office which we see in the New Testament disappeared as *charismata* disappeared; and the charismatic leader (such as Paul and the other apostles) was replaced by the hierarchical administrator who had no *charisma*. How this theory is related to developments in the post-apostolic Church lies outside the scope of this study; it is sufficient here to say that I see no foundation for the theory. But the distinction which Harnack made has often been implicitly accepted in theory or in practice, and the theory permits us to point out a few consequences of the idea of authority as an operation of the Spirit.

It is clear that the New Testament knows no office in the Church, whether it be an office of authority or some other office which is not charismatic. The minimum level of membership in the Church is a charismatic office. Harnack's view that this understanding of authority disappeared ignores the whole sacramental structure of the Church. It is easy to confound such phenomena as tongues and prophecy with the *charisma* as such. Membership in the Church and membership in the clergy are both achieved by sacramental initiation in which the Spirit is conferred; and to regard this as mere ritual is to degrade the sacramental liturgy to the level of ceremonial display. How do we suppose that the Spirit manifested itself in such operations as teaching or almsgiving? Yet these are operations of the Spirit along with prophecy and tongues. We may forget with Harnack that the conferring of the Spirit empowers one to love according to his office in the Church.

Yet Harnack's theory has found its best support less among Protestant theologians than among Catholics who think of

Church authority as no more than government or administration. The history of the Church shows enough instances in which the power of authority has been developed along other lines than the power of the Spirit. Whether these developments can be included among what we have called legitimate developments of the idea and use of authority is a serious question. I have already suggested that this type of evolution is creeping secularism rather than a development of the use of authority to meet changing situations and new needs. If power becomes anything other than a function of love, it is hard to distinguish it from secular power—secular power directed to a noble end, but still secular in its nature.

Authority is a function of the one Spirit in the one body. We have to consider the relations of authority to the other members of the body, and the relations of the function of authority to other functions of the Spirit in the Church. We can begin with the rare picture of authority at work which we find in Matthew 18:15–18, a passage paralleled in an extremely summary form in Luke 17:3. Here directions are given on how to deal with a brother who has offended. Three steps are recommended: person-to-person admonition, admonition in the presence of two or three others, and finally admonition in the presence of the community (*ekklesia*). If the offending brother refuses to listen to the *ekklesia,* he is regarded as a Gentile and a publican; he loses his membership in the community. The work *ekklesia* occurs only twice in the Gospels, both times in Matthew (16:18 and here). In this passage, "church" is a misleading translation; the word designates the entire community in opposition to the two or three witnesses summoned in the second step. Actually the officers of the Church are not mentioned explicitly. Private and personal measures are recommended in the first two steps, and appeal to the whole assembly only as an ultimate measure. Reconciliation is a personal affair, not something to be achieved through official channels. However, the unrepented offense is a wound in the body of the Church, and if the offender will not mend his ways, he must be summoned before the Church. Obduracy at this point is refusal to accept the way of life of the Church, and the offender has effectively severed himself from the community.

What interests us here is that this disciplinary action, the most severe action practiced in the apostolic Church, is achieved without mention of the officers of the Church. That they are present and active must be presupposed; we have seen and shall see again that the apostolic Church had officers. Paul acts in virtue of the apostolic office when he orders that the incestuous man should be expelled; it should be assumed that other steps had been taken and had failed. In Matthew, the church, meaning here the individual congregation, is a reality which is capable of taking action; indeed, it is the supreme agent. The church acts when all its members participate in the action; and it is total participation which gives the action its solemnity. Authority here is the authority of the church, meaning all its members together. This authority is called "binding and loosing," the terms which are applied to the authority of Peter (Matthew 16:19).

Luke describes the primitive community of Jerusalem as "of one heart and one soul" (Acts 4:32). This community, we have seen, was not formless; it lived under the leadership of the apostolic group. But it is obvious that Luke presents the primitive Jerusalem church as a kind of model and exemplar of the Christian community, and the feature which he chooses to emphasize is its unity of sentiment and purpose. This unity is not achieved by the imposition of the will of the officers of the Church; it is a spontaneous unity arising from the inspiration of the Spirit present in the whole Church. In the only divisive question mentioned by Luke—the question of the admission of the Gentiles and the obligation of the Law—unity is restored by the action of "the apostles and elders with the whole church" (Acts 15:22). As in Matthew, Church authority at work here is the authority of the whole Church, and this is perfectly coherent with the thinking of the New Testament writers; for if the Spirit is present and operative in the whole Church, authority, as a work of the Spirit, must be the function of the whole Church. This does not mean that all the members of the Church have offices of authority, but that each member actively cooperates in the function of authority according to his own *charisma*.

We return now to the Pauline image of the body. This image appears in 1 Corinthians 12:12–28, the earliest and fullest expression of the idea, in Romans 12:4–8, and in Ephesians 4:11–16 (in the opinion of a number of scholars, Ephesians is the work of a continuator of Paul). In each of the three passages Paul refers to functions or offices within the Church. Writing to the church of Corinth with its factions, Paul uses the image of the body to show that all the members of the body need the other members. This analogy of society to a body with interdependence of the members was a commonplace in Greek and Roman wisdom; the Christian image of the body is of another order because the body is Christ. Authority is one of the functions of the Spirit which needs the other functions in order that the function of authority itself may be fulfilled. In a secular society authority is conceived as the central motive function which directs and moves subordinate functions. In the Church direction and motivation is from the Spirit to all the functions of the body; authority is not and cannot be absolute, for authority, too, has its interdependence. Not all members of the body are equal, as Paul is careful to say, but all are equally members, and all move under the impulse of the one Spirit. This imposes in the Church a mutual

respect for all offices and functions. Those who are subject to
authority must respect authority, and those who are in authority must respect those who are subject to authority.

The emphasis in Romans 12:4–8, as we have noticed, is
different. Here Paul uses the image of the body in order to
show that no member should think too highly of himself; it is
an inverse way of saying that each member should respect the
other members. It is easy to conclude from this that subjects
should respect authority, as we have suggested above, but this
is not Paul's intention. All must respect each other. A second
consequence of the image of the body is that each should use
the *charisma* which is his. Failure to use one's *charisma* may
be due to one's indolence or timidity; it can also be due to the
fact that some members of the body impede the *charismata* of
other members. Authority is as much liable to this defect as
any other office in the Church.

Ephesians 4:11–16 conceives the body not as something
achieved, but as something in the process of growth to its full
stature. The passage follows an emphatic statement of the
unity of the Church, as we have noticed, and it goes on to
affirm that diversity of gifts must exist within the unity. The
idea of growth in Ephesians adds the theme that the body
needs all its functions in order to attain full maturity. The
maturity which is attained by the full cooperation of all the
members is "upbuilding in love" (4:16).

The place of authority in the image of the body is rather
difficult to define because authority is given no particular
place. Authority is not the head of the body, for the head is
Christ. It is not the function which controls other functions;
at least this is not said, and the Greek language has a number
of ways in which it could have been said. No control is implied
except the control of the Spirit. Authority is not the unifying
principle of the body; this again is the Spirit. Authority is one
of numerous functions, all of which are necessary for the full-

ness of the body. No member, including authority, can say that it has no need of another member. The place of authority falls into the categories which we have seen in other New Testament terms. Authority is meaningful as a part of a larger whole, the reality of which authority does not determine.

This image cannot be converted into conventional social and political terms. Authority as a function of the body of Christ is a new concept as the body of Christ is a new concept of society. Authority must emerge as a function proper to the body of Christ, not to some other society. Authority is an operation of the Spirit, but it is only one of the operations of the Spirit. Romans 12:3 is addressed to authority as well as to subjects: no one should think more highly of himself than he ought to think, but he should think with sober judgment according to the measure of faith which God has assigned him.

5. Offices
in the Apostolic Church

EARLIER WE TURNED OUR ATTENTION to the apostolic office, because this office is the basic form of authority in the New Testament to which all other offices are related. We must now consider the other offices which are mentioned; in them we see the first steps of the evolution of authority. The pastoral epistles (1–2 Timothy, Titus) and 1 Peter exhibit some special features which justify a separate consideration of these documents. These letters show a more developed structure of authority than we see in other New Testament writings; it is this development, together with other features, which leads most critics to place these writings at the end of the apostolic age and to attribute them not to Paul and Peter, but to continuators. Ephesians also, which is pertinent here, is regarded by many scholars as the work of a disciple of Paul; but its date is less certainly near the end of the apostolic age.

The earliest example of assistant officers is the appointment of the Seven in the church of Jerusalem (Acts 6:1–6). These Seven are not called deacons, but their functions are so close to the functions of the officers later called deacons that no real distinction between the Seven and the deacons is possible. The Seven were appointed to "serve tables"; but it has been noticed that this Greek idiom sometimes means in Hellenistic Greek and in the papyri "to keep accounts." In either sense of the phrase, the Seven were appointed to care for the material affairs of the Jerusalem community; the Twelve were thus freed "for prayer and the ministry of the word" (Acts 6:4). The appointment of the Seven was occasioned by a dispute concerning the care of the widows of the community. The election of the Seven was committed by the Twelve to the entire community; election by the whole church was, it seems, the normal way in which offices other than the apostolic office were filled in the apostolic Church.

Yet Acts 6–8 does not show the Seven limiting themselves to the service of tables. Stephen proclaimed the gospel with so much vigor that he was killed by the Jews. Philip also proclaimed the gospel and baptized, the two functions which have traditionally been the functions of deacons in the Church. Philip was not empowered to confer the Holy Spirit. We have noticed earlier that Luke presents the Jerusalem community as the model of the local church; we must now suggest that Luke was not really familiar with the practices of the Jerusalem church and that this unevenness in the description of the office of the Seven reflects variation of local practice in the primitive churches. The apostles led in the proclamation of the gospel, but they did not monopolize it. Paul often refers to his helpers (Romans 16:3,9,21; 2 Corinthians 8:23; Philippians 2:25 and 4:3; Colossians 4:11; Philemon 1,24), and we can be sure that most of these were "fellow workers" in the proclamation of the gospel. We cannot, however, give an official title to most of them. Nor can we give a definite picture of the part they played in the work of Paul. It appears that their chief assistance was in "teaching," the meaning of which term in the New Testament is discussed in the following chapter.

The language of Paul on offices and functions has a charming ambiguity. In some instances we can be sure that the title used indicates an office in the sense of a stable position filled by election and appointment for some defined service of the Church; in other instances the title may mean not an office, but a function which could be discharged by anyone without a permanent election or appointment. This ambiguity is easily observed in Romans 12:6–8 where Paul enumerates the *charismata* of prophecy, service (*diakonia*), the teacher, the exhorter, the distributor [of alms?], the "president," the almsgiver. All of these terms could indicate an office; none of them, not even "president," does so with certainty. Almsgiving was an important function since certainly one and very probably two functions are mentioned which are connected with almsgiving. The ambiguity in this enumeration may be due simply to the fact that Paul was writing to a church which he did not know personally, and the fluid character of offices and functions did not allow him to speak of the structure of the Roman church in other than general terms. The functions which he mentions were of the sort which would be found in any church, but the offices associated with the functions could vary from one church to another.

Two other lists, parallel at some points, are found in 1 Corinthians 12:28 and Ephesians 4:11. Ephesians is less certainly the work of Paul, but the list in 1 Corinthians represents a church which Paul founded and whose practice he knew. Paul says of the list in 1 Corinthians that God has appointed these in the Church.

1 Corinthians	*Ephesians*
apostles	apostles
prophets	prophets
teachers	evangelists
wonder-workers	shepherds
healers	teachers
helpers	
administrators	
speakers in tongues	

The list in Ephesians is more clearly a list of offices. But are they five distinct offices? The almoners are missing, and they are not clearly present in 1 Corinthians, unless they are meant by the helpers and the administrators (which is highly probable). The list of 1 Corinthians, on the other hand, certainly mixes offices and functions; it is difficult to believe that there were offices of wonder-workers, healers, and speakers in tongues. Nor in Paul's conception of office and function did there have to be offices. In this context Paul is speaking of both office and function as a *charisma,* a gift of the Spirit which issues in an operation; and for his purpose it is indifferent whether the *charisma* issues in a permanent office or a passing function. Both are works of the same Spirit, and Paul is thus enabled to put the apostolic office in the same category with speaking in tongues.

Some other titles which are less frequent in the New Testament have a much longer subsequent history: *episkopos,* overseer (from which the English "bishop" is derived); *diakonos,* lackey (from which the English "deacon" is derived); *presbyteros,* elder (from which the English "priest" is derived). *Episkopos* occurs once in Acts, once in Philippians, twice in the pastoral epistles. The word is used in Hellenistic Greek of the officers of a religious community, and the Hebrew equivalent is used to designate the overseers or supervisors of the community of Qumran. In Acts and Philippians the word occurs in the plural, which indicates that at Ephesus and Philippi the overseers were a college as they were in Hellenistic religious communities and at Qumran. Yet the word designates the chief officer of the local church in the epistles of Ignatius of Antioch, written at the beginning of the second century. Although we cannot trace this development, it plainly occurred before the end of the apostolic period.

Diakonos designates a church officer clearly only in Philippians 1:1 and 1 Timothy 3:8, 12. The functions of the deacons are not specified, but it is obvious that they were the assistants of the *episkopos* (*episkopoi*), and their traditional functions, as we have noticed, are preaching and baptizing, the functions attributed to the Seven in Acts 6–8.

Presbyteros, elder, is not used in a sense which distinguishes it from the institution of elders which appears in ancient Israel, in Judaism, and in most of the ancient world. The elders were the adult males of a town, or city, or of other communities, such as tribes. The assembly of elders was the supreme governing body of the town or the community in local affairs and in the administration of justice. The word occurs in connection with the churches several times in Acts, nowhere in the genuinely Pauline letters, and a few times in the other epistles. In Acts the elders are associated with the apostles in decisions; and this reflects the assembly of the elders in local affairs. The relations of the elders with the overseers are more difficult to define. The elders are mentioned more frequently than the overseers, although not notably more. Some have suggested that the two terms in the primitive churches were synonymous; others, that the overseers were an executive board of the elders. The second view seems much more probable and is more in harmony with the practices of other social units in which elders appear. In summary, it seems that in this area of church office existing structures were adopted, but not without modification; for, as we have seen, the entire idea of leadership in society was transformed by the teaching of Jesus. The apostolic Church had a structure, but the structure was not yet fixed and was open to development. At the top of the structure was the apostolic office which could not be continued because it was founded on the personal call of Jesus. The first development in the structure was to create officers who would replace the gap left by the death of the apostles.

This development can be seen in the pastoral epistles. Bishops, deacons, and elders are clearly offices, and no other offices are mentioned (1 Timothy 3:1–13; Titus 1:5–9). But the ambiguity of bishops and elders is still present. The elders are those in charge (1 Timothy 5:17), and elder and bishop appear to be interchangeable in Titus 1:5–9. There is no sign yet that there is a single bishop in charge of the local church. It seems clear, however, that the elders have become a restricted group; they are no longer the assembly of the adult males. Nothing indicates that these officers were not elected; Titus could "establish" elders in each town (Titus 1:5) by conducting elections, but the ritual conferring of the office was most probably accomplished by the imposition of hands (mentioned for elders in Acts 14:23 and 1 Timothy 5:22, but the rite is easily understood as a general practice). Bishops are established by the Holy Spirit (Acts 20:28), and, as we have seen, the voice of the Spirit was most certainly manifested by the assembly of the entire Church.

The bishops/elders have the care of the Church (1 Timothy 3:4), manage the Church (1 Timothy 5:17), are God's stewards (a title of the apostles, 1 Corinthians 4:1), hold firmly to the sure word as taught, instruct in sound doctrine as well as confute adversaries (Titus 1:7–9), and feed the flock (Acts 20:28; 1 Peter 5:2). The office is, therefore, not merely an administrative office, but a continuation of the apostolic office of proclaiming and teaching. 1 Peter 5:1–5 is a mirror of elders; they should feed the flock not by constraint, but willingly, not for gain, but from desire, not "lording it" over the flock (the same word is used in Matthew 20:25 and Mark 10:42), but becoming examples. It may appear strange that even in the more developed organization of the pastoral epistles we still find an absence of exhortations to obedience to the officers of the Church. This corresponds to the absence of any commission to command given to the officers. We are still in a church which sees the relation of officers and members as a relation of cooperation and harmony in the diversity of functions, not as a relation of superior and subject.

Where do Timothy and Titus themselves stand in the structure of the Church as we see it in the pastoral epistles? Many theologians see in them the first examples of the monarchical bishop. This is slightly premature; they are not identified with any local church, and the local churches, as we have seen, exhibit collegiate rather than monarchical administration. Timothy and Titus appear to be extraordinary officers, carrying on the supervision of several churches as Paul did. It is clear from the Pauline epistles that Paul's fellow workers assisted him in supervision as well as in proclaiming the gospel. By a process which we cannot trace, as we have already noticed, this extraordinary office yielded within a generation or two to the structure which we see in the letters of Ignatius of Antioch.

To what extent is the structure of the primitive Church original, and to what extent is it derived from existing structures? We have noticed that most of the terms we find appear in Hellenistic Greek as designating officers of religious groups. This is not surprising since there are only so many types of office and function in any community, and only so many words to designate them. One has to examine the office and the society in order to see what the word means in each instance and whether the office as well as the title is borrowed. For the New Testament it is established that offices and functions in the Church are new and original, and it has been our purpose to show this in the preceding chapters.

The question of the relations of these offices and functions to Judaism is different. The primitive Church was more closely related to Judaism than it was to any Hellenistic institution. We have noticed that the title "apostle" appeared in Judaism to designate emissaries sent from Jerusalem to Jewish communities abroad. The function of the office is not well known, but, whatever it was, it has nothing in common with the Christian apostolic office except the name. The apostolic office is derived neither from Judaism nor from any other source. The title and office of deacon have no known parallels in Judaism. Overseers and elders, on the other hand, do have antecedents in Judaism and Qumran, and, so far as these offices are administrative, they exhibit no peculiar traits. Administration is administration. It is the transformation of the entire conception of society and its officers which distinguishes the Christian overseer and elder from the Jewish overseer and elder.

There are two Jewish offices whose absence in the Church of the New Testament calls for comment. The word *hiereus*, priest, is never applied to any officer of the Church. The existence of the Christian priesthood is not in question here, but the evolution of the priestly office and of its functions lies outside our scope. Why the title of priest is not applied to the cultic officers of the apostolic Church is most probably explained by the fact that the apostolic Church had no purely cultic officers. The word *hiereus* had a technical sense which made it an improper title for the officers of the Church. Possibly, also, the first Christians were reluctant to use a title which designated the Aaronic priesthood; they did not, at first, think of themselves as competitors of Judaism. Whatever be the reason, the use of the Greek and Latin words for priest in the Church is later than the New Testament writings.

The second missing title is scribe or rabbi. The Church had teachers, as we have seen, and the teaching office will be considered in the following chapter. However, the apostolic Church did not think of its teachers as corresponding to the scribes, the scholars, and teachers of the Law in Judaism. It is easy to understand why the apostolic Church, with the words of Matthew 23 in its possession, would look on the scribal office as something foreign to its own constitution. The scribes had a position of authority and leadership in Judaism which was far out of proportion to their primary function as interpreters of the Law; effectively, they were moral dictators. The

Church found in the words of Jesus and in its awareness of its own mission no warrant for an authoritarian institution of this kind. The gospel was not the Law, and it did not need the kind of interpreters which the Law needed. For the gospel presented a person and an event, not a doctrine or a code of conduct. The person and the event were presented by proclamation, and this meant not only a verbal presentation, but a personal identification of the apostle with what he proclaimed. The ultimate authority was always the living, risen Christ identified with the whole Church. The scribes were an elite clique of experts who had rather well identified their own interpretations with the Law of Moses; the Church had no room for such an elite clique. The Spirit excluded it.

The evolution of Church office exhibits itself in the first place as a distillation of the evangelical and apostolic teaching and practice. The idea and use of authority shows no deviation from the ideal of *diakonia,* of the primary place of the function of proclamation, of authority as an operation of love, of the Church as one body informed by one Spirit. One can see in the pastoral epistles an emphasis upon office rather than upon *charisma.* But office is still a *charisma.* Office is' a function within the Church and not over the Church. The inner reality of the Church endures as the Church expands and as its organization becomes more complex, for it is the inner reality and not the organization which makes the Church what it is.

When we say that the organization became more complex, we should not overstate the complexity. The organization of the apostolic Church was by modern standards extremely simple. We have noticed that the function of various offices is hard to define. This is due mainly to the fact that information is not given, but it is due in part also to the fact that offices had not acquired a rigidly fixed form. The impression which the early Church leaves of itself is that it was very tolerant of variation in form and function; there is no clear deliberate effort to reach fixity of structure. The office and the function can be modified to meet existing situations; there are many gifts, but one Spirit. The structure itself is not sacred; the inner life which gives the structure its Christian character is sacred. It is not surprising that the same flexibility does not appear after the apostolic age; it is no more than natural that techniques which were found useful should be adopted permanently. The apostolic Church was still finding itself; the postapostolic Church had found itself in the main lines of its official structure. But the New Testament shows with great clarity a feature which the later Church has always retained, even though it has been less frequently necessary for the later Church to show this feature—and this feature is the flexibility by which the Church adapts its structure to changes in the history and the culture in which the Church exists. In this area rigidity would be fatal.

6. The Teaching Office

THE TEACHING OFFICE has long been understood to be a part of the mission of the Church, and the nature of "authoritative teaching" has been extensively discussed in theology. The development of doctrine and of practice has been so extensive in this area that we must examine the earliest form of ecclesiastical teaching in the New Testament. Our examination will be brief since the New Testament contains very little material on the teaching office. Certain problems arise because the Aramaic, Greek, Latin, and English words for "teach" are so broad in meaning that ambiguity arises. When the New Testament uses the word *didaskein* (teach) and its cognates, it is safe to say that the words never mean the kind of "authoritative teaching" which is treated in modern theology.

If one consults the concordance of the New Testament, one would conclude that Jesus was certainly a teacher; he was commonly addressed as "teacher." But this form of address is deceptive. "Teacher" (Greek, *didaskalos*) represents the Aramaic *rabbi,* "my teacher." Jesus was called a rabbi because most people knew no other category in which to place him. Like other rabbis, he was followed by a group of students, and he appeared to be teaching an interpretation of the Law. His own disciples used the title in addressing him because it was one of the most respectful titles which one Jew could give to another. But the title "teacher" in no way distinguished Jesus from the scribes, all of whom were addressed as "teacher."

Jesus was, of course, much more than a teacher, but he accepted the title because it did not misrepresent his position in the Jewish community.

The content of the teaching of Jesus is, of course, the entire collection of his words in the Gospels. It is somewhat paradoxical that Mark mentions frequently that Jesus taught, yet gives the content of his teaching much less extensively than the other Gospels. Teaching in the synagogues, which is often attributed to Jesus, was the explanation of the Old Testament. Such an explanation, as we read in the Sermon on the Mount (Matthew 5-7), is a collection of homiletic discourses in which Jesus used the text of the Old Testament as a point of departure for what was new and original in his own teaching. The parables were one method by which Jesus taught. His own Messiahship and, in particular, the mystery of his passion and death were the objects of teaching. This leads us to the distinction between the proclamation of the reign of God and the teaching. The teaching fills out and explains the nature of the reign and the demands of the reign by the use of the Old Testament. In Judaism the only teaching known was the explanation of the Bible, and the word is used in the Gospels primarily in this sense. Teaching, as it was understood in Judaism, was not exegesis in the modern sense of the term. The discourse of the teacher began from the text of the Bible, and the development of the discourse was supported by appeals to the text of the Bible; it was not conceived that a discourse could be conducted outside the framework of the Bible. But the use of the Bible was quite free by modern standards, with generous use of accommodation of the text to the point which the teacher wished to make. Jesus, then, was a teacher in the sense that he spoke within the biblical framework and presented his material as based upon the Bible.

Matthew (7:29) remarks that people were amazed at the teaching of Jesus because he taught with authority (*exousia*) and not like the scribes. We have seen that a more accurate translation of this phrase is that Jesus taught with a commission. It is a subtle way of comparing his discourse with the prophetic discourse, which is the word of the Lord, rather than with the discourses of the scribes. Although the scribes also taught with authority, they based their authority on their fidelity to the text of the Old Testament, beyond which they felt they could not go. Actually they went far beyond the text at times, but the theory of scribal teaching was that it proposed nothing which was not contained in some way in the Law. With Jesus there came a new revelation of the word of God; he taught with a commission as Moses and the prophets had taught with a commission.

Teaching is mentioned often of the apostles. The commission given in Matthew 28:18–20 is given in virtue of the universal authority which Jesus has received from the Father; it is a commission to make disciples everywhere. "To make disciples" is explained as two actions: to baptize and to teach the baptized all that Jesus had commanded. The emphasis on what Jesus commanded is a part of the pattern of Matthew's gospel. This Gospel, more than the others, presents Jesus as a teacher and interpreter of the Law who proposed a code of conduct with specific instructions. The Herodians hypocritically say that he teaches the way of God in truth (Matthew 22:16). The entire New Testament conceives the gospel as a way of life; Matthew's presentation of the way of life bears more resemblance to the Jewish presentation of Judaism under the Law as a way of life. This, along with other reasons, justifies interpreters in calling Matthew the most Jewish of the Gospels. The apostles are commissioned to teach nowhere else in the Gospels.

The apostles did teach, however. The object of their teaching was Christ (Acts 5:42), the word of the Lord (Acts 15:35), the word of God (Acts 18:11). Apollos, although not commissioned, taught the things about Jesus (Acts 18:25). All these phrases, including the sentence about Apollos who is described as a man learned in the Scriptures, suggest the same object of teaching which we observe in the teaching of Jesus; it is the explanation of the person and mission of Jesus in Old Testament terms. The purpose of the apostles' teaching was to show that Jesus is the Messiah of the Scriptures, and thus to explain what "Messiah" really meant. The teaching is joined to the proclamation as argument and explanation. Through the application of the Bible to Jesus the apostles derived deeper understanding of his person and mission and a fuller perception of the meaning of the Christ event for the Christian way of life.

That the Scriptures were the object of teaching is less clear in other passages. What Paul means by "my ways in Christ" (1 Corinthians 4:17) may have been clear to the Corinthians, but it is not clear to us. Paul thought that this was an important part of his teaching. In 1 Corinthians 14:6 teaching is enumerated at the end of a series of types of charismatic discourse: revelation, knowledge, prophecy, teaching. The teaching in Colossians 1:28 and 2:7 has no object mentioned. The object of teaching in 2 Thessalonians 2:15 is traditions. We do not mean to imply that teaching in the apostolic Church was exclusively the explanation of the Messiahship of Jesus in biblical terms. But it appears that this was the central element of the teaching from which excursions were made into other theological areas. In Colossians, for instance, the object of teaching is the person and mission of Christ; in 2 Thessalonians it is the *parousia,* which is certainly related to the central element.

This background gives the necessary explanation of the function of official teachers who are mentioned several times in the New Testament. These passages have already come under our notice in other connections. At Antioch there were

prophets and teachers (Acts 13:1). Teachers are listed with
other officers in Romans 12:7, in 1 Corinthians 12:28, and
in Ephesians 4:11. If we are correct in our understanding of
the teaching, these officers were men learned in the Old Testament whose function was to explain in biblical terms the
person and mission of Christ and the Christian way of life.
They must have been specialists. They were not an elite clique,
like the Jewish scribes, for they did not exercise the kind of
domination which the scribes exercised and which, as we have
seen, is repudiated in Matthew 23. But their work was necessary. The official teacher need not have been a specialist in
the sense that he did nothing else; distinct offices and functions
do not indicate distinct persons in the apostolic Church, and
apostles were also teachers. But if we try to define teaching as
a function, the most probable understanding of the function is
that which we have given here.

The pastoral epistles show a concern for sound doctrine
and an awareness of deviations which do not appear in the
other epistles, another indication that the pastoral epistles
come from a later and more complex stage of development in
the Church. There are warnings against teachers of unsound
doctrine (1 Timothy 1:3–7 and 6:2–5; 2 Timothy 4:3–4;
Titus 1:9–14 and 3:9). These passages do not anathematize
unsound doctrine. Those who propose the opinions contro-
verted are members of the Church, and the author (or authors) of the pastoral epistles does not read them out of the
Christian community for these deviations. Most of the unsound
doctrines appear to be efforts to introduce certain aspects of
Jewish belief and practice into Christianity. The authors speak
vigorously against these deviations, but they do not use terms
such as those which the early ecumenical councils used against
Arius and Nestorius. Nor do they use terms like those which
occur in the same pastoral epistles concerning those who have
departed from the faith (1 Timothy 1:19–20 and 4:1–3; 2

Timothy 2:17–18). We see again the distinction between the proclamation and the teaching; it is the teaching and not the proclamation which is affected by the unsound opinions. It is in a sense opposed to this type of doctrinal deviation that adhesion to sound doctrine, particularly to sound doctrine supported by tradition, is urged in the pastoral epistles (1 Timothy 4:6, 11–16; 2 Timothy 4:1–2; Titus 1:9, 3:9). The sure foundation of sound doctrine is the Old Testament Scriptures, the base of New Testament teaching (1 Timothy 4:11–16; 2 Timothy 3:14–17).

In New Testament terminology, teaching is not described as one of the primary functions of the Church. The primary operation we have encountered several times: the proclamation of the gospel, which is also called preaching or evangelization. This operation is nearly synonymous with bearing witness to Jesus. The gospel is the announcement of the arrival of the reign of God in Jesus Christ. The teaching is an important but subsidiary activity; it is the explanation of the gospel. The teaching is not proposed with the imperative necessity which belongs to the gospel alone; it is not the word which saves. We have called it a specialized function. Like all functions and offices in the Church, it derives its meaning and value from the primary function.

We have observed that the evolution of the teaching office from its New Testament form exhibits a degree of modification which is really unparalleled. It is not possible within the scope of this work to trace this evolution in detail. Plainly such an evolution calls for more extended comment, and it will be our purpose to treat this in a subsequent chapter.

SUMMARY

The preceding examination of New Testament texts seems repetitious, and I have not attempted to recast the material in a way which would conceal the repetitiousness. By such a slavish rather than imaginative arrangement two features of the New Testament treatment of authority can be perceived more clearly. One feature is that the New Testament really has little to say about authority in the Church; this, of itself, is important. Church authority is not a dominant theme in the New Testament; it is much less conspicuous than it has been in theological literature for several hundred years. The second feature is that the New Testament texts which touch authority, written by different authors over a span of some decades, all converge on a few simple ideas. The synthesis of these few ideas gives us the New Testament idea of authority, not formally set forth anywhere in the New Testament. At the risk of one more repetitious but brief section, let us recapitulate these ideas.

The New Testament is anti-authoritarian in a proper sense. It abhors that type of domination which in the New Testament world was seen in secular power or in religious autocracy. It is anti-authoritarian in the sense that it permits no member of the Church to occupy a position of dignity and eminence; the first in the Church must be the lackey and the slave of others, and may strive for no dignity and eminence except in dedication to service in love. The New Testament uses words to describe Church officers which place them on the lowest social level known in the Roman-Hellenistic world of the first century. Authority in the Church must depart from the accepted forms of authority and find a new way to exercise itself. It must reflect the person and mission of Jesus Christ.

The nature of authority in the Church and the use of authority are determined by the mission of the Church, which is to proclaim the gospel. Authority is empowered to act within the terms of this mission and within no other terms. The mission of proclamation is the mission of the whole Church; it does not belong exclusively to the organs of authority in the

Church. Authority exists within the Church and for the Church; authority does not determine its own constitution. Authority is one of the operations of the Spirit, one of the organs of the body. The full life of the body, moved by the Spirit, demands the healthy function of all the members; no one member, even authority, may assume functions which are not its own.

Authority in the New Testament is conceived in a way which must be called democratic rather than absolute. Authority in the Church belongs to the whole Church and not to particular officers. The New Testament is strangely silent both on commissions to command and on exhortations to obedience and submissiveness to Church authority. If exhortations to submissiveness are addressed to anyone in particular, they are addressed to the officers of the Church. Both the idea and the use of authority in the New Testament show no signs of rigorous control of the members by authority. Since the mission of the Church is the responsibility of all the members of the Church, all members have a concern in the exercise of authority.

Authority is a gift of the Spirit; as such, authority is subject to the supreme gift of the Spirit, which is love. Like all functions of the Church, the exercise of authority is a function of love. This means that love is directed to persons, not to ideas, or institutions, or things. Authority finds the object of its love in the persons who are the members of the body of Christ; it is impossible to love Christ detached from his body and its members. Love is the supreme motivation both of the officers and of the other members of the Church; with this motivation, anything like a power structure is forever excluded from the Church. Love is the only power which the New Testament knows.

The commission of Christ to his Church imposes on the Church the task of creating new forms and structure for an absolutely new type of society. The new forms which the Church exhibits are based on the union of the Church with Christ and the unity of the members in the body of Christ and in the indwelling Spirit. Only by such a new type of authority can the Church fulfill a mission which has no parallel and no precedent elsewhere.

Part II. REFLECTIONS

7. Leadership

IT IS NOT THE PURPOSE of this study to present a raw confrontation of Church authority in the New Testament with Church authority in the twentieth century. Such a confrontation would be unfair. The obvious external differences might blind us to the inner continuity. Church authority in the twentieth century is derived from the New Testament through a long and complex historical process of development which lies outside our scope. One mistake would be to think that this process has ended. Another mistake would be to think that the development has been unilinear and uniformly progressive. Some developments have certainly been illegitimate; many of these have been recognized as illegitimate and have been abandoned. Other developments can be recognized as legitimate only if the process by which they arose is considered. A bare confrontation which ignored the realities would probably issue in no more than a strident invective against existing authority. The existing authority is not above criticism, but a mere recital of where it deviates from the New Testament would not be constructive. What is needed now is an examination of the use of authority to determine how the mission of the Church and its *charisma* of authority can be preserved in a world which has moved so far from New Testament times. This task is, of course, too great to be resolved in these few pages. It demands the collective wisdom and experience of the Church; and by the Church I mean the whole Church, not only the officers of the Church. Authority is not a notably objective critic of itself. These reflections on authority, stimulated by the New Testament, are intended as no more than a small contribution to a large enterprise.

Our first reflection is concerned with the function of authority in the Church. If we ask ourselves what is the function of authority, our instinctive answer will be: command. This is our instinctive answer because it arises from our experience of the idea and the use of authority in other societies. Yet, a little reflection shows that this is not the function of authority, but one of the means by which authority achieves its end. In the family the end of authority is to rear children to maturity; in the State the end of authority is to procure the common good. Command and obedience are among the means by which the end may be achieved, but an authority which knew no other means than command would surely fail of its end. In a given situation, command may not only be an inept means toward the end, it may positively interdict the attainment of the end. When this happens, the only moral response to a command is disobedience.

The function of authority in the Church of the New Testament, we have seen, is the proclamation of the gospel and the administration of the sacramental system. These two operations establish a community. In the community the operations are continued, the proclamation is enlarged by the teaching, and the regular sacramental ritual demands a structure of liturgical officers and worship. Within the community there is an interchange of active love. The local church is the living continuation of the service of Jesus toward the needy, and one of the major functions of the community is to see that the goods of its members are shared. Not only goods but services are involved; the Church has been too long familiar with that type of "charity" which gives its goods but withholds itself. Unless there is a personal exchange, active Christian

love does not meet its fulfilment. Active love is an essential
part of the proclamation; active love is that aspect of the
mission of the Church which most clearly involves all the
members of the Church and which least needs supervision.

Within this structure, what has authority to do? There are
a number of words which we associate with authority: command, direction, control, and the like. These associations do
not come from a carefully elaborated theory of authority; they
arise from general human experience which moves men to
think of authority in the first place as a restraining influence
and of freedom as the absence of restraint. Yet we have seen
that such words as restraint, command, and control are just
the words which the New Testament does not associate with
authority in the Church. A new type of authority emerges to
suit a new type of community; if we are to apprehend the
reality of this authority, we shall have to find words other than
those which we are accustomed to associate with authority.

Since we are dealing with words which have a magic all
their own, let us see whether the word "leadership" is not a
more accurate capsule description of the idea and the use of
authority in the New Testament than such words as "government" and "control." The Church finds its fulfilment in the
realization of the Christian life in its members. There is
scarcely any point in the New Testament which is less ambig-
uous than the proposition that the Christian life of the members
of the Church is achieved through the personal decision of
each member. No one, neither those in authority nor anyone
else, can make this decision for another. The Christian realizes
his destiny as a Christian because he wills it, not because
someone else has willed it for him.

But the Christian cannot achieve his Christian destiny by
himself, for the fulfilment of the Christian life is simply beyond
the powers of nature. One is enabled to live as a Christian
by his incorporation in Christ. This means that he achieves

his personal destiny in and with the community of the Church; each member assists the other members, and each member has it within his power to make it difficult for other members to realize their destiny. Jesus spoke severely of scandal. The Christian has the indwelling Spirit to guide him and move him; without the Spirit he cannot even say that Jesus is Lord. Much less, then, can he rise to the highest of the *charismata* of the Spirit, the fullness of Christian love. The Christian has the gospel not as a piece of dead literature, but as a living reality in the Church. In the gospel in the Church he apprehends the living Christ, living in the proclamation and in the life of the Church which is one with him. By identification wth the living Christ the Chritian becomes what he is.

Authority certainly has its part in this process, and if authority is fulfilling its own function, this part will not be small. Both Bishop John J. Wright and Thomas Corbishley have called our attention to the fact that authority ought to be a positive force.[6] If authority is merely restraining or coercive, if it is conceived as a principle by which things are not done rather than by which things are done, it becomes purely negative. The best that authority can hope to accomplish by a negative function is to prevent evil; and a negative approach will not achieve even this. To have positive force, authority must have a positive purpose to be attained by positive means; and what purpose can Church authority as such have other than the purpose of the Church itself; and what means other than those which Jesus himself used and communicated to the Church? Authority cannot coerce or compel the Christian to fulfill his Christian destiny. It cannot, by an imposition of its will, command an act of love. What authority can do is to show the Christian what the Christian life is and to move the

[6] John J. Wright, "Conscience and Authority," *The Critic* 22 (1964), #5, 11–28; Thomas Corbishley, S.J., "Power and Authority," *The Way* 3 (1964), 285–293.

Christian to desire the fullness of this life. Authority will do this not by control, but by the full proclamation of the gospel. The full proclamation of the gospel means more than the office of preaching. Authority proclaims the gospel even more effectively by exhibiting in itself the Christian life to which all members of the Church are called. If authority does this, it shows leadership; if it does not do this, it does not matter how much command and control it exercises. Proclamation by action is true leadership, and it is the only kind of leadership recommended in the New Testament.

If one wished to be captious, one could maintain that the texts which give *diakonia* as the function of authority and which liken persons in authority to lackeys and children not only do not recommend command and control, but positively forbid it. Whether this thesis could ever be sustained or not, it is plain that the contemporary Church is not ready for a dicussion of this thesis; it is plain also that a simple adoption of the thesis would produce instant chaos in the Church which we know. What is to be sought is not administrative chaos, but a transformation of the idea and the use of authority; and it would be absurd to pretend that such a transformation can be accomplished instantly. But is it not absurd to think of such a transformation as an ideal which the Church can begin to realize?

It may be urged—and probably will be—that my presentation of Paul's use of apostolic authority not only in the Corinthian letters, but in other letters as well, has been one-sided. There are texts which I have not quoted (such as 2 Thessalonians 3:12) and which sound as much like a command as anything ever uttered anywhere by anyone. In the more developed Church of Hebrews (13:17f) we encounter a rare exhortation to submission. The presentation may indeed be one-sided, but it has never been necessary to show at length that Church authority claims the power of com-

mand. My point is that a person who shows the type of
leadership which Paul showed may also essay to employ the
type of command which Paul employed. For Paul's use of his
authority to set up ordinances and to decide questions must
not be isolated from his conception of the apostolate as a
whole; and it needs no argument to show that Paul did not
conceive of the apostolate primarily as authority to command.
In Paul's thinking it was the proclamation of the gospel, not
command, which was the basic function of the apostolic office.
Let us recall that the proclamation of the gospel was a service
of love, which means that it was a service of persons.

Paul, as we have seen, let no gap appear between himself
and his congregations. His relations with them were personal,
not impersonal and administrative. Is it not at times pathetic
to see administrators make futile efforts to pretend that a
personal relation exists when everyone concerned knows quite
well that it does not? Like a true leader, Paul wished his
congregations to share his will, not to be subdued by it. What
they do not accept with understanding and sympathy, he seems
to think, they will not accept at all—at least they will not
accept it in the way which will assure Christian decision. Authority in a secular society does not need to urge and entreat;
Paul thought himself above neither. His decisions are shared
actions as far as he can make them such.

All well and good, one may say; but Paul is a unique figure,
and smaller men must do things in another way. This is true,
but disturbing. The factor which made Paul great and not
small is still present and active in the Church: the Church is
still the body of Christ in which the Spirit dwells. Small men
do not become great by continuing to do small things in a
small way. One small thing which Paul never does is to insist
upon his authority to command even when he is defending
his apostolate; and all small men can easily imitate him in this
restraint. Paul shows none of the insecurity which small men

show when they fear that someone may not obey them or may conceive a better way of doing things. Paul was simply unconcerned about his position, or his dignity, or his power over other men; he was a *diakonos*.

We have given enough attention to Paul's Corinthian correspondence; a glance at his epistle to the Philippians shows him as an apostle in another light. There is no perceptible occasion for this epistle; the church of Philippi had no problems of belief or discipline (except that Evodia and Syntyche seem to have had a falling out); it asked no questions; it was in no trouble. Paul wrote the letter simply because he and the Philippians liked each other, and he wished to keep in touch with his friends. As an apostle, he took the occasion to repeat the proclamation of the gospel without rebuke or imperiousness. In unconstrained confidence he reveals how much he was identified with that which he proclaimed; we have to postulate a rare personal relationship which enabled him to say to the Philippians naively, "Do it the way I do it" (1:19–26 and 3:3–17).

It may appear utopian to think that the type of leadership shown by Paul could be transferred to a Church so far removed in space and time and so changed in size and complexity. Before we assume that Paul was working on a very simple and a very limited scale, we should locate his epistles and his churches on the map. Paul was in touch with more than a dozen churches scattered from the interior of Asia Minor to continental Greece. We do not know how large the membership of these churches was, but when we consider the means of travel and communication which Paul had available, we are astonished at the way he kept track not only of the Church, but of individual members of the churches. We are less astonished when we reflect that Paul kept track of people because they were his primary interest. He knew that the Church is the body of Christ and that all members of the body are persons. He probably had as much reason as any modern administrator to plead that the task of knowing and loving people as individuals, and still get his work done, was too much for him. To Paul, knowing and loving people as individuals were his work.

For the type of leadership which we see in Paul is given only to individual persons, not to a faceless mass. Personal relations make authoritarian control impossible; and authoritarian control sustains itself by depersonalizing its subjects, by reducing them to a mass, and the mass to a thing. Things can be guided, controlled, coerced; persons can be led. Paul knew nothing of objective and detached management; he knew that, when one is personally involved, objective detachment is impossible. He may even have thought—if the question ever occurred to him—that objective and detached administration of persons is a sin against love. Personal identification with the gospel meant personal identification with those to whom the gospel was proclaimed. He became all things to all men and thus gained all; but he also made his own their personal griefs and problems. Bad management, the modern efficiency expert would say; but it was great leadership. The military services warn their officers against "over-identification" with the command, because personal involvement makes it extremely difficult to send men on a mission of which death is the certain issue. Paul would scarcely have thought that this cultivated insensibility can be transferred to the Church. It is part of the apostolic office, as it is of Christian love in general, to bear the burdens of all. It is part of the apostolic office to die—daily, if necessary—not to dispatch others to death. I think many of us have lost the understanding that personal involvement is an essential component of Christian leadership and one of the elements which makes it distinctly Christian; it is love under another name.

The size and complexity of modern churches certainly demand forms of leadership which the apostolic Church did not need. The Church can evolve these forms without abandoning apostolic leadership. An administrative structure is accessory to authority in the Church; it is not authority itself. But churchmen can easily adopt an administrative structure which has been devised for other than ecclesiastical purposes. The Church in the course of its history has reflected the features of the absolute monarchical state, the feudal state, the army, and, in modern times, the corporation. Although the Church has yet to reflect the features of the democratic or the republican state, there is no reason to think that it will not. The vice of administration in all these forms is that it deals better with things than with persons, and it deals best with persons when it treats them as things. Administration is, by definition, detached, objective, and unaffected by personal considerations. Unless it is transformed by love, it has no place in the Church. Administration can easily become an end in itself rather than a means. The structure of administration tends to take on a sacred character the longer the structure survives.

It hardly seems necessary to add that the transformation of the Church into a power structure is not a confirmation of authority, but a perversion of authority. The power of the Church, we have seen, is the power of love. Authoritarian power is foreign to every line of the New Testament in which authority is mentioned. The Church has experienced corruption in many forms; it has known simony, nepotism, concubinage and other vices. But these forms of corruption are possibly more tolerable and less harmful to the mission of the Church than that corruption by which the Church is made a means for men to wield power over other men. The use of power in the vulgar sense of the imposition of one's will on another is in direct opposition to the sayings of Jesus in which this form of self-assertion is forbidden formally and explicitly. Power is not a substitute for apostolic leadership. Power is not even an inferior way of achieving the end of apostolic leadership; it is a way of not achieving that end. But men adopt the way of power because they feel that true leadership is beyond their capacity. Apart from the possibility of graceful resignation when this incapacity is recognized—a course of action not often enough considered—there is the other possibility of growth to the stature of true leadership. This growth is the work of the Spirit, not of human talent and industry.

Archbishop Roberts has given one of his essays the felicitous title, "On Commending Authority."[7] This is a duty of which the bearers of authority must always be conscious: the duty of commending authority, of making it attractive, of meriting the love which is owed authority. Authority commends itself in the ways which we see in the New Testament. It commends itself by not asserting itself, by persuading and convincing rather than by coercion, by leading rather than by dominating, by being personal and not impersonal, by dealing with those whom it governs as partners and fellow members rather than as subjects. Authority commends itself, most of all, by sincere active love, a love which rises from an understanding that, when one loves the faithful, one loves the Church; the Church is not something different from its members. Yet it is easy to think that authority is commended just because it is authority—which is to say, because it is power. Those in authority can forget that a person who is respected only because of his power is not really respected at all; he is feared or despised.

I have spoken of authority as leadership rather than as government; and in speaking in these terms I have not diminished the responsibility of authority. I think I have rather increased it. Leadership can make demands and get them which mere government can neither make nor get. Leadership appeals to motives which are beyond the reach of obedience

[7] *Black Popes* (New York: Sheed and Ward, 1954).

as such. Leadership does not impose its own will, but creates an active union of wills. Our concluding reflection here can be that, while government of the Church is vested in its officers, leadership is vested in all its members. It is the practice of the Church to propose for public veneration men and women who best illustrate the fulfilment of the Christian ideal; most of these men and women were truly leaders. They were not all members of the hierarchy, nor were they appointed to other governing or administrative offices; or, if they were, it was often after they had shown leadership without such an office. It is unfortunately true that the two *charismata* of leadership and office are separable; not all leaders are officers, and not all officers are leaders. Perhaps we have not often enough reflected that leadership is a responsibility of officers, that government and control are not enough. We shall return in another chapter to the leadership exercised in the Church by those who are not officers, for one of the problems of the Church has always been the reluctance of some of its officers to admit any leadership which is not either official or officially controlled.

At the time of this writing it is less than a year since the Church in the Second Vatican Council has solemnly promulgated its most recent statement on its own authority.[8] This document will furnish ample material for study and interpretation and—like most conciliar statements—for theological disputes for a long time to come. Speaking, no doubt, with that degree of personal prejudice which leads one to see his own views in ecclesiastical documents, I believe this statement moves in the direction of a leadership founded on the New Testament. The statement does not renounce the traditional threefold division of the episcopal office into sanctifying, teaching, and governing, nor should this be expected. The direction of these essays is not to abolish government in the Church, but to suggest

[8] Butler and Baum, *The Constitution on the Church of Vatican Council II* (Glen Rock: Deus Books, 1965) 98–118.

some directions in which thinking and practice may move. The
Council has stated at length some ideas on the collegiality of
bishops which express with sufficient clarity the sharing of
decisions on the episcopal level. It states without ambiguity the
primacy of the office of proclaiming the gospel for the bishops,
and it is in terms of proclamation that the teaching office is
defined. It reaffirms the truth that the Roman Pontiff and the
bishops are spokesmen of the Church as no one else can be.
It notes that the bishop is the chief liturgical officer of the
diocese who leads his people in worship. Its description of the
governing office of the bishop places the emphasis on the pastoral quality of his government rather than on its jurisdictional
quality.

In subsequent discussions it may emerge that the most important part of the statement of the Council is none of these,
but its reaffirmation of the base of the power of Church government in the power of orders. We have noticed above that
in the New Testament every Church office is a charismatic
office. The *charisma* is conferred on the officers of the Church
in the sacrament of orders. If the priest and the bishop fulfill
their office duly, they do it not in virtue of a grant of power
from a superior ecclesiastical officer, but in virtue of the Holy
Spirit who is given them. There may be ultimately no better
statement of the difference between authority in the Church
and secular authority than this.

8. The Prestige of Authority

THERE IS A PHENOMENON in the contemporary Church which has not yet been noticed by many writers, for good and obvious reasons. It has been noticed, however, in the conversation both of the clergy and the laity, and it is a phenomenon which warrants serious concern if it indicates more than isolated trouble spots. The phenomenon is this: ecclesiastical authority has been losing prestige. This statement may seem to be in flat contradiction to the veneration in which the late Pope John XXIII is universally held, outside the Church as well as within it, a veneration which had led some to suggest that he be canonized by acclamation. Yet it is possibly John XXIII who delivered the most telling blow to the prestige of ecclesiastical authority at a time when this authority had been under fire to a greater degree than most people realized. He did it simply by departing from the established image of ecclesiastical authority and by projecting a new image against which all prelates have been measured. He did it by openly voicing his own impatience with ecclesiastical bureaucracy and ecclesiastical pomp loathed by many Catholics who were reluctant to express their mind about things which seemed to be so completely identified with the Church. He did it by summoning an ecumenical council with the explicit intention of "bringing the Church up to date" (*aggiornamento*) and thus implying—and that not subtly—that the Church was enough out of date to need *aggiornamento*. Here he again voiced a sentiment silently cherished by a great many Catholics. And perhaps he did it most of all by making it clear, both in the preparations for the Council and in its first session, that the Church was ready for a complete examination of itself. John XXIII was a prelate with whom the faithful could identify themselves. They were not accustomed to this.

Yet a diminution of the prestige of ecclesiastical authority is not to be attributed to John XXIII alone. How, one may properly ask, is this diminution of prestige manifesting itself? Because one could honestly say that he simply has not noticed it, I regard it as my duty to single out some areas in which prestige has been lost. For one quite obvious point, the hideous question of segregation has hurt the American hierarchy no matter what position they took. Our American bishops have been openly criticized; they have in some instances faced open rebellion both for taking a stand in favor of integration and for not taking such a stand. The utter paradox of a situation in which both attitudes are blamed reflects the utter irrationality of the whole controversy over segregation. It also reflects something else. Many others besides the bishops have lost prestige here; neither political leadership on the national, state, and local levels nor leadership among the lower clergy and the laity has covered itself with glory. In such a situation the bishops whose stand has been unambiguous and supported by action have been outstanding, and they are more than a few. It is pure hindsight, and I apologize for saying it, to observe that a firm and even severe position accepted and implemented by *all* the American bishops—had it been taken some years ago—would have enhanced ecclesiastical prestige. Had this been done, we should not have been afflicted with the untenable proposition that what is moral in one diocese is immoral in another. Morality should not change its patterns from diocese to diocese. Again, it is hindsight to observe that no compromise was possible with a monstrous evil and that local customs and traditions cannot determine basic Christian morality. None of us were very quick to see this, even those whose learning and influence should have placed them in the front rank. When the whole Church in America did not support a firm position, however, moral leadership passed into other hands.

A second point. It seems that the long smoldering problem of birth control is about ready to burst into flame. We are just beginning to discover how many of the laity have found intolerable the moral imperialism of the clergy; the laity could have quoted Matthew 23:4: "They bind heavy burdens, hard to bear, and lay them on men's shoulders; but they themselves will not move them with their finger." The problem is not the rigorous morality which has been commonly taught; Catholics expect their moral teaching to be rigorous. It was, rather, the emphasis on this single moral problem (almost to the exclusion of other problems), the pushing of the morality of marital relations to a key position in the Christian moral structure which it does not have. It was the cool abstract discussion of theoretical principles entirely detached from the living reality of marital union which the laity know by experience. It was the apparent refusal to seek any real alleviation of a really serious burden. Now that the ironclad thesis seems likely to be at least re-thought and restated, the victims of the ironclad thesis feel some resentment—not hard to understand—against those who presented the morality of birth control with hardly less clarity and cogency than they presented the morality of murder. A thesis which needs re-examination and restatement, they think, should have been presented with more reserve in the first place.

Here the prestige of ecclesiastical authority has been diminished not by timidity and compromise, but by refusal to compromise. Prestige was not strengthened by the fact that the hierarchy and the clergy were rigid in their treatment of birth control, where they were dealing with Catholics, and flexible in their treatment of segregation, where they were dealing mostly with non-Catholics. Prestige was diminished by refusal to take the layman and the laywoman seriously as responsible Christian adults with a genuine concern for Christian morality. Authority lost prestige because authority appeared to be autocratic, whether it was or not; the faithful recognize by the illumination of the indwelling Spirit that autocratic government is foreign to the genius of the Church. Prestige was diminished because authority appeared to manifest no understanding or sympathy, or—to return to a phrase used earlier—because it seemed to be more concerned with things than with persons. Prestige was diminished because authority seemed to show in its moral judgment a distorted moral perspective in which deviations in sex are viewed as cutting more deeply into the life of the Church than refusal to love. Many of the laity think that the clergy, convinced in their hearts that even the legitimate use of sex should be discouraged, have no genuine interest or concern with the problems of those who do not lead a celibate life.

A third point in the diminution of ecclesiastical prestige is the growing awareness of uses of ecclesiastical power which can most euphemistically be called arbitrary and autocratic, less sympathetically unjust and vindictive. The clergy have known of these defects in the use of power, but they have usually felt that loyalty to the cloth (identified in their minds with loyalty to the Church) forbade the revelation of these things even to their brother clergy. Concealment is no longer possible. Writers have been forbidden to write when nothing censurable has been found in their writings. Speakers have been forbidden to speak when nothing reprehensible has been found in their utterances. Teachers have been dismissed from their posts without explanation and reinstated without explanation. The public has become aware of processes in ecclesiastical offices which resemble the Star Chamber or the councils of Cesare Borgia more than they resemble the assembly of the *agape*. The public somewhat stubbornly adheres to its belief that no one hides things except those who have something to hide. The public sees no motive for the secrecy which envelops so much of ecclesiastical administration except the fear that the administration would be ashamed of some things if the secrecy were lifted. Somehow an image has been created of vast power concentrated in the hands of a small clique of career administrators who work under the cloak of anonymity and whose decisions seem to come under the review of no one. If the image is false, then no effort should be spared to destroy it; but as long as this image persists, clerical prestige suffers.

A fourth point in which the prestige of authority is diminished is the unhealthy relation of ecclesiastical authority to political authority, particularly in Spain and in many Spanish-American countries. I call this relation unhealthy from a North American point of view, because Protestant controversialists have for some years thrown Spain and Latin America at American Catholics as the true image of Church-State relations in a Catholic country. Furthermore, enough theologians in the Catholic world support this interpretation to cause embarrassment. The usual response of American Catholics is to say that the Spanish way is not the American way, but by this answer we implicitly reject the policy of the Spanish and Latin American hierarchies and refuse to identify ourselves with their understanding of the character and the mission of the Church. When we do this, we compromise episcopal authority; or is it we who compromise it? Whoever does it, episcopal authority is compromised. The Second Vatican Council's statement of religious liberty will enormously enhance the prestige of the Church for the right reasons. It is still too recent for us to forget the loss of prestige which the Church suffered when this declaration was delayed in a previous session.

Yet a fifth point can be mentioned as involved in the loss of

ecclesiastical prestige. Ecclesiastical pomp and ceremony are
viewed, more and more, with hostility that is not always con-
cealed. Few Catholics are discontented with the pomp and
ceremony of worship, but more are discontented with the
pomp and ceremony which surround the person of the clergy-
man outside his cultic functions. Without realizing it, Catholics are expressing their awareness of the difference between
such pomp and the simplicity of the New Testament. It is true
that the faithful flock to pontifical ceremonies; it is also true
that the Basilica of St. Peter is one of the few places in the
world where one can see a full-scale live reproduction of the
pageantry of a Renaissance court. One can understand why
our predecessors thought that spiritual authority should be in-
vested with an external splendor which symbolized the dignity
of authority. We can understand it, even if we think they were
wrong in adopting the trappings of secular princes. One should
also be able to understand the impatience of modern people
with these antiquated trappings. Modern people live in a world
where the state uniform of the head of the most powerful
nation in the world is a business suit—and it is in the same
garb that other heads of state appear. Even in the armed services, which are second only to the ecclesiastical profession in
the love of pageantry, the general wears little to distinguish
him from the private soldier in combat; the magnificent dress
uniforms of generals and admirals are becoming more and
more rare, and they are scarcely worn except at formal balls
and diplomatic receptions. When the secular State can dispense
with the symbolic apparatus of royalty and nobility, it seems
that the ecclesiastical polity, which has in its foundation documents a warning against such apparatus, could even more
quickly dispense with it. Originally devised to increase prestige, ecclesiastical pomp is now helping to destroy that which
it was intended to support.

Connected with ecclesiastical pomp is another factor in the

diminution of prestige. The pomp is a symbol of power; the more grandiose the pomp becomes, the more effectively it symbolizes the base of power. It is a commonplace in sociology that power rests on an economic base. As a general principle, people have that degree of freedom which they can afford; economic dependence limits freedom and power. Jesus instructed his disciples to achieve freedom by independence of economic need; they would be free because they were poor by choice. The pomp of the ecclesiastical state is a concrete indication of the economic security on which ecclesiastical authority reposes. Where authority has the wealth which renders it independent, authority is able to exercise the power of wealth; it need not appeal to the kind of power which is peculiar to authority in the Church. If authority is identified with the wealthy ruling class, it has a share in that type of power which is called plutocracy.

This is not intended to be a complete enumeration of the things which can be considered partly responsible for the diminution of the prestige of ecclesiastical authority; but these are samples which seem to admit no denial. It can be argued that the loss of prestige of ecclesiastical authority is a part of the social development of our times; that authority of all kinds, parental as well as civic, is losing prestige; that the loss of ecclesiastical prestige is simply another manifestation of the spirit of independence and rebellion which is the mark of our restless world. And it would be foolish to assert that general social conditions have nothing to do with the condition of the Church. At the same time, the alleged spirit of independence and rebellion must assert itself in a world which has seen a tremendous growth in totally authoritarian political government in the last generation. It should be noticed that the loss of prestige occurs in countries which have no notable tradition of disobedience, and rebellion, and lawlessness; and that the loss occurs among the older generation, which is presumably more conservative, as well as among the younger generation. If the modern trend toward personal independence—which seems to have been arrested, if it is not being reversed—has something to do with the loss of ecclesiastical prestige, it has not everything to do with it. One suspects that the appeal to "the independent spirit of the age" is made by those who do not wish to admit that ecclesiastical authority may have contributed to the loss of its own prestige.

The points mentioned above suggest that authority has contributed to the loss of its prestige. The points suggest that authority has exhibited the opposite defects of timidity and autocracy; that it has used means unworthy of the end of the Church; that it has raised itself above its proper level. This last item is of such importance that it will receive a more extended reflection in the following chapter. Authority has adhered to antiquated forms. No doubt, a more tolerant response to these things from the faithful and from non-Catholics would have prevented the loss of prestige or, at least, would have lessened the loss. An atmosphere of mutual tolerance, which both the bearers of authority and its subjects must work to sustain, would be a token that the Church lives in the spirit of the New Testament. Authority should, to use Archbishop Roberts' phrase, commend itself by its authentic manifestation of the living Christ. Authority in the Church, if the promises of the Gospels are fulfilled, can expect to be misunderstood, and reviled, and persecuted. These things authority cannot avoid. What authority can do, however, is to see that it is reviled and persecuted for the right reasons.

No Catholic can view with equanimity the loss of prestige of Church authority. Authority has a necessary function in the Church which cannot be fulfilled by anyone else. The Church continues to operate if authority is deficient in its function; but the Church does not operate as well as it does when authority is acting responsibly. The instinctive reaction of many Catholics to the loss of prestige is to hide the evidence, to reassure themselves and anyone who will listen to them by affirming that it is all a pack of lies. But they do not convince others, and perhaps they do not even convince themselves; and such defensive Catholics should know that no problem is solved by concealing or distorting the truth. No Catholic is really surprised when he finds that Church authority is human and shows its humanity in crass and obvious ways; he is surprised when he is told that authority is really superhuman and therefore free to act in an entirely human manner. Authority does not lose prestige by revealing its human weakness so much as by pretending that its human weakness is something else.

Our concern, therefore, is not removed by assurances that there is no cause for concern. We do not seek for authority that type of prestige which is proper to civic and political authority, and we are happy when Church authority does not have that type of prestige. We are concerned if authority seeks civic and political prestige; we are more concerned if authority seeks this type of prestige and fails to attain it; and we are most deeply concerned if it seeks this type of prestige and gets it. We are concerned because authority belongs to the Church; no member escapes pain when another member suffers. Our service to authority is to sustain it in being what it ought to be, and here we must return to the New Testament. But we cannot sustain authority in any way unless it is agreed that authority is the concern of the whole Church, not the exclusive concern of its officers.

9. The Values of Authority

WE HAVE SEEN that the New Testament does not define closely the competence of Church authority. The New Testament sets forth the end of the Church and the means available for the end; but it leaves the application of the means to the discretion of the Church in particular situations. Such a general commission could be construed as a grant of absolute power, were it not for the restraints imposed upon authority by the constitution of the Church and the principles of the Christian life. The restraints have not always been clearly perceived, and this leads us to the problem of the excessive esteem of authority and its powers.

Excessive valuation of authority is certainly connected with the loss of prestige which we considered in the preceding chapter. Authority loses prestige more quickly by failing to meet its obligations than in any other way. Over-valuation creates both in the minds of officers and in the minds of others an exaggerated idea of the competence of authority; and when authority cannot rise to exaggerated demands upon its powers, it loses respect. Such exaggerations are particularly damaging to Church authority. On the one hand, the failure of authority to meet the demands made upon it can be attributed to a failure of the Spirit which acts in the Church. On the other hand, if authority assumes a wider scope than it is competent to govern, it does not encroach upon the actions of men, but upon the action of the Spirit within the Church. In the words of Paul (Romans 12:3), authority then thinks more highly of itself than it ought to think, and not with sober judgment. A false ideal of the competence of authority is built in the mind of the members of the Church, and they are disappointed when authority, as it must, fails to rise to the ideal.

The Church is a divine institution; and the conclusion that authority in the Church is divine authority is easily drawn. A further corollary that authority in the Church is identified with the deity is drawn less easily; but when members of the Church are urged to see God in the officers of the Church and the will of God in the commands of authority, there is very little difference for practical purposes. The principles that one should see God in one's superiors and God's will in their commands are venerable in the traditions of the Church; but the venerability of these principles does not protect them from misunderstanding. A false identification of authority in the Church with the deity will go as far as anything conceivable can go to damage the prestige of authority; for men are not God, and they do not succeed well when they attempt to play God.

The Church is a divine institution, and authority in the Church is a part of the divine institution. This truth must be preserved together with the truth that the entire structure of the Church, including the lay state, is also a divine institution. Authority does not exist by a divine institution different from the institution by which the Church as a whole is established. Jesus did not establish authority first, and then give authority a church to govern. We have noticed that the New Testament excludes a false duality between the Church and authority in the Church. To think of authority as a special divine institution not so much in the Church as over the Church is certainly to set up a false duality. There are different gifts, but one Spirit.

It is altogether true that the members of the Church should

see Jesus Christ in the officers of the Church, just as the officers should see Jesus Christ in the members. It is the presence of Jesus Christ in the members of the Church which is the basis of the Christian community of love. All members owe to Jesus Christ in other members the *diakonia* of love; and this duty is laid upon the officers of the Church more explicitly than it is laid upon the members. Imposition of one's will is a strange form of *diakonia*. Equally strange is the application of the line, "He who hears you hears me" (Luke 10:16; see Matthew 10:40), to the commands of obedience; in the context the line clearly refers to the proclamation of the gospel, and Luke places the line in the discourse to the seventy-two disciples. The whole Church is the body of Christ, and the identity of the Church with Christ cannot be restricted to a part of the Church, nor affirmed of any part of the Church in a special way. If the identity could be so restricted or affirmed, we should have a church within a church; or we should have full members and associate members. We should have the Spirit exclusively mediated to the Church through authority in the Church. All of these things are out of harmony with the New Testament. Authority does represent God; but authority does not represent God's power, his knowledge, or his wisdom. Authority does not assume the divine providential government or the divine attributes. Authority represents Jesus Christ as the subject and the object of love; and this representation authority shares with all members of the Church.

Even deeper issues are involved in the principle that one should consider that the acts of authority are the acts of God. No theologian or ascetical writer who states this principle omits the reservation that this consideration ceases if authority commands something sinful; obedience ceases also, and disobedience becomes a duty. The possibility that authority can command something sinful must not be regarded as purely speculative. But the possibility totally negates the principle that the acts of authority should be considered as the acts of God. For the acts of authority cannot be considered the acts of God until it has been shown that they involve nothing sinful, and this means that the acts of authority are subject to the review of the individual person. But the acts of God are not subject to the review of anyone; and the analogy breaks down at this vital point.

One ought to be ready to adjust one's Christian life to error, incompetence, and even malice in the bearers of authority in the Church. The Christian response to these things is tolerant and forgiving love, a readiness to help authority to overcome its faults, and a sincere resolution to carry on the work of the Church if some in authority should fail to fulfill their function. God is not the object of tolerant and forgiving love; we attain God as the object of love by tolerance and forgiveness of the human beings with whom he has identified himself, but we do not direct tolerance and forgiveness to him. These reservations upon the acts of authority as the acts of God are serious. The principle of identifying the two may indeed make obedience easier in most instances; but it makes obedience nearly impossible in just those instances which on all accounts are most difficult, and the principle may blind one to the duty—rare, we hope—of disobedience. God has not guaranteed the Church immunity from the incompetence and malice of its officers. The Christian response to these things is not to cherish the incompetence and malice of the officers. To say that the individual person secures his own spiritual integrity by unthinking obedience, whatever be the consequent damage to the Church, is a remarkably anti-social and solipsistic view of one's responsibility to the Church.

False identification of authority with the Church makes authority exclusively responsible for the mission of the Church. In such a false identification the individual member is absolved from any personal responsibility except for his own personal welfare. His own welfare is then reposed exclusively in his obedience to authority. There is no warrant for this way of salvation anywhere in the New Testament. The recent Eichmann trial disclosed a deep and distressing social illness in our society. Eichmann's plea of innocence was that he did what he was told, and that no one should be blamed for obedience. This plea was rejected not only in a court which had doubtful jurisdiction over the crime, but also by world opinion. Yet world opinion in other instances rewards unquestioning obedience to orders, the action for which Eichmann was judged guilty. Eichmann's crime was really not his obedience to orders, but the fact that he obeyed on the losing side. One would like to see a clearer difference, on the one hand, between Eichmann's idea of obedience and the principle that obedience to Church authority is obedience to God, and, on the other, between Eichmann's plea that the obedient man is innocent of moral responsibility and the principle that one is saved by obedience, whatever else may be involved. One hesitates to say that the principle is a solvent of morality; at the same time, it is certainly not a safe moral principle taken by itself. The reservation that authority has no power to command something sinful means nothing if it is agreed that authority is the supreme judge of the morality of its own actions.

One may say that the spiritual danger involved in the apotheosis of authority is remote, and I trust it can be granted that it is remote. But a remote great danger is still great; and I have remarked that the danger is more than purely speculative. Experience forbids us to regard the danger as unreal. But this danger is, to be sure, more remote than other dangers which are implicit in the excessive esteem of authority; and some of these dangers deserve mention. How the idea of authority in the Church as an omnicompetent body arises is difficult to say; probably both authority and members cooperate in bringing this distorted idea to birth. Authority contributes to the idea by assuming more and more functions; the members contribute by abdicating to authority their own responsibilities.

The competence of authority is traditionally defined in theology as faith and morals. These two terms sum up the activity of the Christian life. One cannot quarrel with the use of these terms; one may quarrel vigorously with some of the ways in which the terms have been understood. The two terms refer primarily to the teaching office of the Church; and this office has become so closely identified with Church authority that we shall have to give it separate consideration in the following chapter. Here we shall speak in more general terms; and we may approach the problem by recalling the distinction so often made between government by law and government by men. Government by law is regarded as the ideal of political society. Law means that the limitations of government are set down precisely, and the competence of government defined with equal precision. By law, the means which the government may use to achieve its end are enumerated, and the use of means other than those approved is an abuse of power. The transfer of such a constitution to the Church appears attractive. Yet we have seen that one of the greatest dangers which the Church faces is assimilation to secular power. When I ask whether the authority in the Church is a government of law or a government of men, I ask a question which the New Testament does not answer formally.

I suggest, however, that the New Testament describes a government of men and not a government of law. The positions occupied by the men to whom authority in the Church is committed are not like the offices of civil government. Law insures the citizens against the arbitrary and unjust use of power. The Church insures her members against such abuses by denying to her officers the kind of power which can be abused. She insures herself by effecting a transformation of the persons who bear authority—a transformation no different from the transformation which the Church effects in all her members, the incorporation of all her members in Christ. This transformation enables the officers of the Church to bear authority worthily, and it enables the members of the Church to render Christian obedience to authority. Love, not law, is the basic constitution of the Church; if love fails, law is no substitute.

Yet the Church does have law. One may argue that this is a necessary part of the evolution of the Church. But there is a difference between having law and governing by law. Law is impersonal and objective; law has just those features which it seems authority in the Church should not exhibit. Law inhibits the freedom both of members and of officers; and law appears to be not entirely in harmony with the loose idea of authority which the New Testament conveys. Jesus and Paul both state emphatically that the gospel liberates from the Law of Judaism; they do not say that the Law of Judaism is removed in order that another law no less rigorous and controlling should replace it. In the New Testament it is Jesus himself, and not a code of precepts, who replaces the Law in the scheme of salvation. Incorporation into Jesus Christ is, with difficulty, converted to subjection to a legal code. Law is not intended to regenerate men, but to protect men from the intolerable consequences of their unregenerate nature. If the Church has law, law can be only a remote accessory to the central mission of the Church; the mission remains above and outside the concept of law. The government of the Church, I propose, is a government of men and not of law because it is formally and expressly a fraternal government; the union of love allows no other idea of authority in the Church.

Law in the concrete consists in much more than a few broad and general directions which are implemented by the discretion of those who are governed by the law. There is a spirit in law by which law grows; the law is applied explicitly to more and more particular situations until the directions of the law can become almost totally controlling. Here the idea of authority in the Church as omnicompetent finds room to enter. Do not the faithful generally assume that no activity in the Church can be properly initiated or pursued without the approval of Church authority? And do not the faithful think that approval in modern times means supervision as close as the officers who are concerned wish to make it? The contrast between the broad commission which Jesus gave his Church to proclaim the gospel and the detailed directions which now exist for the conduct of even the simplest organizations within the Church is striking. Parkinson's Law operates as well within the Church as it does in secular organizations.

So many people have said privately, and a few publicly, that the Church is excessively managed that the remark seems hardly worth repeating. Some implications of over-management, whatever be the extent to which it exists, deserve notice. Over-management is a vote of non-confidence in the ability of the members of the Church to fulfill their own office in the Church. Over-management implies that the Spirit is mediated to the members of the Church only through the official organization. Over-management supposes that the Church lacks a sufficient number of intelligent and responsible members; and, if the Church suffers this lack, no bureaucracy, however large and well organized, can make up for it. Over-management expresses a doubt that the Church retains the power it has by its constitution of producing a number of men and women who can initiate, plan, and execute without constant detailed directions from an ecclesiastical officer. Paul had no doubt that the apostolic Church had this power. What has the Church lost since apostolic times?

Over-management can come both from officers and from other members, as we have seen. The argument most frequently alleged in defense of over-management is the duty of officers to protect the Church and its members. No one can quarrel with the legitimacy of this purpose, but one can ask whether protection is the primary end of authority. In New Testament terms, protection is clearly not primary. A certain amount of risk is involved in the mission of the Church to proclaim the gospel. One can eliminate this risk by not proclaiming the gospel. Protection which guards the members of the Church as if they were retarded children or chronic invalids protects them, but defeats the purpose of the Church. Protection of the Church against herself is paradoxical. Protection which treats the members as if they were thieving servants or intruders in the Church does little credit either to the members or to the officers. If the reservation of decision to Church officers did assure the protection of the members of the Church, such reservation would still be contrary to the New Testament idea of authority. But experience forbids us to believe that reservation of decision to Church officers does protect; in particular, it fails to protect the members from the officers. Experience shows that the officers of the Church deserve just as much confidence as the members of the Church, no more and no less. And why should the officers deserve more or less confidence? There are different gifts, but the same Spirit.

Over-management, again without reference to the degree to which it actually exists, can obscure the central mission of the Church. We have seen that in the New Testament the central mission of the Church is the proclamation of the gospel and the administration of the sacraments. The officers of the Church are, first and foremost, apostles; the word of God is their ministry, not the service of tables—recalling again the recent exegetical hypothesis that the phrase "service of tables" may mean the keeping of accounts. The Church has not entirely escaped the journalese designation of administrative positions as "top jobs." The modern bishop inherits an administrative structure and an enormous burden of diversified responsibilities which he is not free to unload. He suffers more than anyone else from the fact that, in the minds of many, he is a manager rather than an apostle and a minister of the word and the sacraments. His suffering is compounded by the harsh reality that he must combine the function of management and the function of ministry, both of which are full-time responsibilities. Most of us do not appreciate how well this combination is made if it is made at all. Bishops suffer from their awareness that their position as presidents of corporations often hinders their personal engagement with the flock which they feed. The modern version of the episcopal office is a problem which needs serious examination, and this examination will be best conducted by those who have the office and who know best its problems and its responsibilities.[9] We may be sure that this examination will be among the first tasks of post-conciliar commissions and that the other members of the Church will support the task in all ways which are available to them.

In addition to the perplexities which the bishop faces—and the same perplexities face those who occupy positions of major responsibility in religious communities—management has created a new class within the Church: the staff of religious superiors. The Vatican staff under Damasus consisted of Jerome and a few amanuenses. There is scarcely a diocese in the Church today so small that such a staff could get the work done. It would be highly unrealistic to think of annihilating bureaucracy because when any common effort, whether in politics, business, or religion reaches certain dimensions and complexity, bureaucracy is the only way in which it can be administered. Joseph A. Fichter has sketched the inherent conflicts between the bureaucratic structure and professional

[9] How well this can be done can be seen in *Continuum* 2(1965, Winter) in articles by Bishops Dwyer, Hallinan, Hammes, Hodges and Mussio.

structure; both structures are necessary, but the conflict seems to be, as I have called it, inherent.[10] It is difficult to appreciate fully the dedication of those clergy who accept assignment to the bureaucracy and to admire sufficiently the success with which they find in this work a fulfilment of their professional ideal. As a group, they are skilled and affable—indeed, they often include some of the best talent in a diocese or a religious community. It is usually from this class that bishops are selected.

Yet they form an administrative class, and their point of view and judgment will most probably be the view and judgment of administration. The administrative class, like the professional class, has its occupational blind spots. The professional may see the details, but not the large picture; the administrator may see the whole picture, but not the details. Of necessity, administration deals with things rather than with persons; its concern is the business of the Church, not its mission. As the business grows more and more complex, disengagement from the mission is something which must be resisted. It can become difficult to assess the needs of the mission and the resources we have to fulfill the mission. Excessive valuation of authority leads to excessive valuation of administration; and this can lead to a too little valuation of the apostolic ministry. One has met administrators who conceive of the apostolic ministry as the pedestrian and the routine work and who regard those who do the apostolic work as the hewers of wood and the drawers of water in the temple. The "top jobs" exist on the bracing level where decisions are made.

The problem of over-management is that too many decisions are made on this bracing level. Instead of administration, let us return to the idea of leadership. The administrator organ-

10 Joseph A. Fichter, S.J., *Religion as an Occupation* (Notre Dame: University of Notre Dame Press, 1961) 219–233.

izes and directs; the leader does and invites others to do with him. There is a type of leadership as rare within the Church as it is outside the Church for which, it seems, we can strive.[11] Leadership knows the capacity of its men and puts them to tasks of which they are capable; by its own mysterious magic it elicits from them just a little more than that of which they are capable. It furnishes them with means to accomplish their task rather than with elaborate directions on how to do it without means. It creates in them that confidence which is gained only through the knowledge that one is trusted. It leaves as wide a field as possible to their judgment and decision, restraining them only when it is necessary to keep their judgment and decision from colliding with another's judgment and decision; and it assumes that they, too, are aware of the possibility of collision on a crowded road. It accepts the fact that an intelligent and experienced man is at least as much of an expert on how a task should be done as a superior officer who is removed from the realities of the task—if indeed the superior has ever engaged in the task. It accepts these men as full partners in the venture, honoring them by believing that their concern for the integrity of the Church and the success of its mission is equal to one's own concern. Something like this, I submit, is apostolic leadership; I am not sure that anything else is.

I do not think that this use of authority would diminish the prestige of authority. If Church authority has been losing prestige, in the last analysis it is because authority has here and there failed to be truly ecclesiastical. Authority will not lose further prestige by becoming all that it ought to be and ceasing to be what it ought not. The members of the Church will fully

---

[11] One can profitably read Thomas Corbishley, S.J., "Power and Authority," *The Way* 3(1963), 285–293; Fichter, *Religion as an Occupation* 243–279.

support authority in which they recognize the features of apostolic leadership; they are entitled to look for these features in Church authority. Those who are restive under control could become enthusiastic when they learn that they are not servants, but friends (John 15:15). Love, even disorganized love, is a far greater power than discipline; it is love, not discipline, which Jesus recommended to his Church as the bond of unity.

10. The Teaching Office

WE OBSERVED EARLIER that the teaching office of the Church must receive special consideration. In modern times the teaching office has grown to far greater dimensions than we see in the New Testament. The development of authoritative teaching is extremely complex, and we risk some misunderstanding by passing over the history of this development. Although this historical study would take us far beyond the scope of this work, at the same time it does not seem possible to omit the teaching office in a discussion of Church authority.

Our survey of the New Testament has revealed a different conception of the teaching office from the conception to which we are accustomed. The teaching office in the New Testament is subsidiary to the office of proclaiming the gospel, and, in fact, teaching seems to mean the specialized work of explaining the gospel in Old Testament terms. When we look at the teaching office in the modern Church, it is at once apparent that the teaching office is a development of the office of proclamation; but in the development the function of teaching has been expanded far beyond what we see in the New Testament. The very fact that the word *magisterium* is the technical term for the office shows how the concept of the office has changed, for the Latin word, *magisterium,* signifies the office or function of a schoolmaster. The necessity of development, we repeat, is not under discussion, but the fact of development should be noticed. The modern idea and use of the teaching office is not identical with the New Testament idea and use of the office of proclamation.

The gospel is not a doctrine, by which I mean that it is not a body of knowledge. The New Testament contains no doctrinal synthesis. Christian scholars of later times have prepared syntheses; the scholars of Alexandria in the third century have the honor of being the first to apply philosophical methods to the study of the New Testament. The Christological heresies of the fourth and fifth centuries arose from the misapplication of philosophical terms to the Incarnation, and the Church was able to correct these deviations only by finding an accurate application of philosophical terms. Under the stimulation of these discussions, Greek philosophy became part of the standard equipment of the Christian scholar; and with Greek philosophy came the Greek genius for systematic thought. But the variety of syntheses of New Testament theology in ancient and in modern times shows that the New Testament is somewhat stubborn in resisting systematization. Each age forms its own synthesis, which yields to another synthesis; the syntheses are determined more by the philosophical context in which they are written than by the contents of the New Testament.

The gospel is the proclamation of a person and an event, and a call to a personal response to the person and the event. This was the gospel in New Testament times, and it is still the gospel. The gospel did not depend on Greek or Jewish learning either in those who proclaimed it or in those who heard it. The response demanded was faith, not knowledge or understanding. When the Church developed to the point where it counted learned men among its members, it became apparent that the faith of the learned man is a different response from the faith of the unlearned. But the difference does not lie in the essential nature of faith. The gospel is still proclaimed to learned and to unlearned; and learning is not a prerequisite for faith either in its beginning or in its fulfilment. The learned man is no more at home in the Church than the unlearned. The Church asks of her members the degree of knowledge of which they are capable, and in some instances this is not much. But such uninstructed members of the Church are still full members; and the uninstructed can show insights into the faith which escape the learned.

It may appear that I am presenting an anti-intellectual view of the faith. It seems necessary, however, to justify the place of the unlearned in the Church in order to justify the place of the learned. No one has ever really questioned the place of the unlearned in the Church; a number of people have questioned the place of the learned, both in the past and in the present. For the past, let the classic spiritual work of Thomas à Kempis represent the extreme.

I would rather feel compunction than know how to define it (1, 1.3).

Cease from overweening desire of knowledge; because many distractions are found there, and much delusion. Learned men are very willing to seem wise, and to be called so. Many are the things which it is of little or no profit to the soul to know (1,2.2).

The humble knowledge of oneself is a surer way to God than deep researches after science. Knowledge is not to be blamed, nor simple acquaintance with things, good in itself and ordained by God; but a good conscience and a virtuous life are always to be preferred. But because many take more pains to be learned than to lead good lives, therefore they often go astray, and bear no fruit at all, or but little. Oh, if men would be as diligent in the rooting out of vices and grafting in of virtues as they are of mooting questions, there would not be so many evils and scandals among the people, nor such laxity in monasteries! Truly, when the day of judgment cometh, it will not be asked of us what we have read, but what we have done; not what fine discourses we have made, but how like religious we have lived. Tell me, where now are all those doctors and masters with whom thou wast well acquainted while they were yet alive and in the glory of their learning? Others now hold their preferments, and I know not whether they ever think of them. In their lifetime they seemed to be something, and now they are not spoken of (1,3.4–5).

I think anyone who gives this much attention to learning—these passages are only samples—has a deep, dark suspicion that learning is not a legitimate activity. Thomas à Kempis is emphatically certain that no one is a better Christian for being learned—so emphatically that he implies that one is an inferior Christian if one is learned. More recent criticisms of learning and the learned move in a different direction; the learned are suspect not because of their learning as such, but because their learning is an attempt to advance beyond the learning of the past. To the learning of the past the word "doctrine" is applied with that peculiar unction which means that because learning is old, it is official—or at least semi-official.

There must be a clear distinction between faith and doctrine. Faith is the response to revelation; doctrine, the product of theology, is an understanding and an application of the faith. The Church must have both. Doctrine is more secure the more closely it adheres to the sources of faith; the introduction of other elements is never done without some risk. But the risk has to be taken; for doctrine which does not interpret the faith in the light of learning is not doctrine, nor does it explain and interpret. Doctrine is subsidiary to faith now as it was in New Testament times. The Church uses theology and doctrine; indeed, these are the means by which the Church evolves with the world and with history. Faith never becomes antiquated; doctrine very easily does. Theology has served the Church well at some times, poorly at others. In the long view, it appears that the Church has had more bad theology than good theology, nor is bad theology necessarily a theology full of errors. Theology is bad when it is timid, when it refuses to be creative and even venturesome, when it refuses to advance from fixed positions, when it becomes stagnant, when it refuses to meet actual problems—in a word, when its first objective is safety. Safety can often be attained only by advancing. One does not avoid moving vehicles by remaining in their path. One can avoid them by not entering the lanes of travel; but then, of course, one would never get across the street. The analogy has some value. Without good theology, the Church cannot continue to make the proclamation immediate and urgent to men of all countries and times.

I said that the Church uses theology; but historically theology in the Church has been a private rather than an official enterprise. Whatever we expect from Church authority, we do not expect creative thought from it. We do expect creative thought from Christian intellectuals, and we expect the officers of the Church to incorporate the solid work of these intellectuals into their own office of proclamation and teaching. During most of her history the Church has recognized that her intellectuals must be left free to do their own thinking in their own way. It is here that the problem of Church authority in the teaching office and the relations of the teaching office to learning come into focus.

What is the function of Church authority toward learning? It would appear at first glance that Church authority could have no function toward any learning other than theology; we know that historical evolution has carried us far beyond this point. The Church is empowered to proclaim the gospel and to explain it. What the Church, as the Church, possesses, she possesses by revelation; she is the living word because she is the body of Christ. By her commission the Church is certainly empowered to tell what the gospel is and to distinguish true from false gospel. She is empowered to determine whether an explanation of the gospel is accurate or inaccurate. Those who explain the gospel are officers of the Church; as such, they are under the supervision and the direction of the Church. The type of supervision which the Church can exercise over her teachers is perhaps the most obvious illustration of the type of direction which I outlined in the preceding chapter: a supervision characterized by freedom and mutual confidence rather than by suspicion and close surveillance. It should be a relation of friends and colleagues, not a relation of hostility or neutrality.

Among other things, we need a history of intellectual freedom in the Church and the use of ecclesiastical authority toward learning. Up to recent times the supervision exercised by authority was loose rather than strict. Previous censorship of manuscripts is a modern development, and not an entirely wholesome development. How control became tightened is a complicated story not yet fully told. One factor was certainly the theological revolution of the Middle Ages which coincided with the intellectual awakening of western Europe. The theologians of the Middle Ages took all learning for their province; disciples of Aristotle, they had attempted to write an encyclopedia of Greek learning. Thus the distinction between theological theses and scientific propositions was blurred. With the Reformation came attacks on Church authority (in particular, the teaching authority) and on many theological theses. At the same time the natural sciences emerged from the control of metaphysics and found their own methods. I summarize a great intellectual movement in a few lines here, and the summary is obviously incomplete; but it is not my purpose to write a history of thought from Thomas Aquinas to Francis Bacon. I intend merely to enumerate the factors which made it possible for the officers of the Church to commit the greatest doctrinal blunder in the history of the Church; the condemnation of the heliocentric cosmology of Galileo.

This blunder is a classic because it illustrates almost every conceivable feature of how not to administer the teaching office of the Church. That Galileo was right for the wrong reasons is irrelevant; the commission of cardinals which forbade him to teach was wrong for the wrong reasons. The commission implicitly affirmed its competence to decide questions of secular learning and to decide them without investigating the problem or the evidence. It applied theological methods and theological argument to a problem which is not theological. It adhered to unhistorical and uncritical interpretation of the Bible. It refused to accept the progress of learning. It involved faith in questions which have nothing to do with faith. Worst of all, it exhibited arrogance. One would think that this abuse of power, for which the Church has been apologizing ever since, would have taught some lessons on the administration of the teaching office. Yet the Church barely escaped a similar scandal concerning the hypothesis of evolution much more recently.

Somehow from the New Testament to the early seventeenth century the Church had become, in the minds of some of its officers and members, the depository of all learning and the final arbiter of all questions. It should be evident that this is not a legitimate development of the office of proclaiming the gospel. Jesus gave his Church no commission to control the world of learning. Yet this caricature of the teaching office still persists in the Church. Some solemnly proclaim that the Church has "the truth" with the obvious implication that the Church has all the truth and no one else has any of it—and this despite the fact that the Church has never been free from a generous number of theological errors cherished not only by her members, but also by her officers. Not every theological error corrupts the gospel—fortunately. The infallibility of the Church is limited, but the limits are often ignored. When spokesmen of the gospel proclaim something else than the gospel, they are safe from error by the same means which any one uses to secure himself from error: the examination of the evidence and the restriction of statements to what the evidence permits. The spokesmen of the Church can be safe from error in such cases by using the means which were so blatantly flouted in the case of Galileo and by most nineteenth-century theologians who wrote on the hypothesis of evolution.

Some find it annoying to have the nose of Church authority rubbed in the Galileo case so frequently. However, it does seem necessary to draw attention to this unsavory mess every so often because the mess shows so clearly that when Church authority ventures into the world of learning, it goes outside the area of its competence as Church authority. Church authority is not empowered or equipped by its constitution to enlarge learning or to dispense it. Learning can serve the Church, and it has served the Church magnificently; but learning does not serve the Church as the slave of the official class. Church authority, when it deals with learning, must respect learning with its content, its principles and its methods. Learning, unless it receives due respect, cannot serve the Church.

It can be urged that the idea of the Church as the sole custodian and dispenser of all knowledge is indeed a caricature which no one has ever seriously maintained. Perhaps no one has maintained it in so many words, but we have approached the caricature often enough to be concerned. Church officers have been known to express disapproval of certain learned theses of which they evidently knew next to nothing. The Church is competent to pass judgment on learning where learning manifestly denies the gospel; and experience shows that a manifest denial of the gospel is not hastily to be assumed. Beyond this, the teaching office of the Church has no competence in learning. The Church can affirm that a learned thesis is wrong only because the thesis contradicts the gospel, but the Church has no power to write the correct thesis. The Church can reaffirm and define its belief, but this leaves the problem of learning just where it was. While very few think of the Church as the compendium of all knowledge, many more than a few are reluctant to admit that there is any area of knowledge in which the Church is not empowered to make decisive statements. This is a kind of ecclesiastical imperialism which needs restraint. The Church has not the mission of answering every question which her members may ask; and it is more than a trivial disservice to her members to let them think that she has.

We have observed that the area of the teaching office of the Church is traditionally defined as faith and morals. The moral teaching of the Church deserves special attention. The New Testament contains much more material which could be classified as moral than it does of material which could be classified as dogmatic. The gospel proclaims a new way of life and institutes a moral revolution. Primitive Christians needed to see the impact of their belief on their conduct, and the New Testament makes this impact clear. Indeed, the full impact of the moral revolution has not been felt even yet. We still have much to learn about the depth of the transformation in human conduct which Jesus Christ has wrought.

The moral revolution does not take the form of law. Judaism offered a very detailed code of instructions on conduct; the gospel frees men from the Law. It also frees men from the principle that conduct is a matter of law. The moral proclamation is the revelation of a new life motivated by new principles and guided by new insights into the moral possibilities of man regenerated in Christ. The individual Christian must realize this transformation in his own life; the New Testament does not seem to conceive that detailed instructions are possible. Nor are they necessary. When the Christian is incorporated into Christ, the life of Jesus will realize itself in him.

Elizabeth Anscombe has proposed the interesting thesis that morality is not the object of doctrine like the sciences. She concludes that there is really no moral revelation in the proper sense of the word.[12] She draws our attention to the distinction between authority to command, which is the imposition of one's will, and authority to impose one's belief. Moral teaching is not command, and the imposition of moral belief does not directly touch conduct. The moral principle is always abstract and general; the moral act is always concrete and particular. The only moral teaching left, Miss Anscombe concludes, is teaching to do. This, I submit, is the kind of moral teaching which we find in the New Testament. The New Testament presents a concrete reality which can be reproduced in action.

Yet, just as many members of the Church think that the Church owes them an encyclopedic compendium of knowledge, so also many think that the Church owes them detailed instructions on how to solve every moral problem. These good people should, they think, have to make no decision without the assurance that the Church has already made the decision for them. Is the teaching office of the Church empowered to give this kind of direction? Can the Church furnish this spiritual security? A brief glance at the evolution of moral teaching in the Church will help us to grasp the problem.

It took the Church hundreds of years to reach a clear position on the morality of slavery. The Church retained its teaching on the immorality of usury some time after the revolution of capital made the teaching antiquated. A number of the Fathers and later theologians show their conviction that the sexual act in marriage is venially sinful. If St. Thomas More had taken direction from the majority of the English hierarchy, he would have accepted the Act of Supremacy. The Church gave its blessing to the aggressive religious wars of the Crusades; in modern times it still has to speak without reserve on

[12] "Authority in Morals," in *Problems in Authority* (Baltimore, Helicon Press, 1962), 179–188.

the morality of nuclear warfare. I referred earlier to the problem of birth control as one of the reasons why authority has lost prestige; we can now inquire more closely why prestige has been lost. A moral proposition, supported a generation ago by several arguments, has suffered the erosion of each of these arguments. The clergy know the difficulty of imposing an obligation on the faithful when the clergy have no clear and obvious explanation of why that which is forbidden is wrong. Now the clergy find themselves saying equivalently, "We used to tell you that birth control is against the Bible and against the natural law. We can no longer tell you that it is against the Bible. The explanation of how it is against the natural law is too complicated for us to give you. Now we tell you it is wrong because we have been telling you that it is wrong; and if we withdraw from this position, the infallibility of the Church will be compromised." Whatever be the ultimate issue of this moral discussion, the position both of the clergy and of the laity at the time of this writing is intolerable.

If one speaks of limits in the moral teaching of the Church, they will not be the same limits which we find in other areas of doctrine. Yet there must be limits; and perhaps one of our major tasks, of which we are not yet really aware, is to find these limits. There is nothing in the nature of moral theology which would prevent a Galileo case in the area of morality. If we do not find limits, we shall be forced into the impossible position of furnishing a complete and detailed code of conduct for every member of the Church in every situation—which is to say, we shall become the scribes of the new law. We clergy show a reluctance to say to anyone, "That is your moral problem, and it must be solved by your decision." If we say this to anyone, we feel that we have failed in our duty, and the Church has failed in us. But has the Church failed if it has proclaimed the basic message of Christian morality? Is the distinction sometimes blurred in our minds between the proclamation of Christian morality and the management of the lives of other people? The faithful can make mistakes in moral judgments; it must be remembered that total submission to clerical direction will not insure the faithful against mistakes in moral judgments. They will make our mistakes instead of their own.

It seems clear that the more the teaching authority of the Church moves into details in moral instruction, the farther it moves from its commission. It will be protected by the charisma of infallibility, but the examples noticed above suggest that this charisma sometimes operates slowly. The Church is commissioned to teach the morality of the gospel, which is the moral revolution of Christian love. The New Testament reduces all morality to the commandment of love.[13] This implies no commission to teach philosophical morality, although moral doctrine must be formed by the use of reason. Reason, however, must operate within the morality of Christian love, not outside it. If authority solves a moral problem by philosophical reasoning rather than by the application of the gospel, its position has no more strength than its philosophical reasoning. It will be as strong or as weak as an ecclesiastical commission met to settle the question of whether the sun moves round the earth. Quite possibly a moral problem which cannot be reduced to love is not within the competence of the teaching office. Jesus refused to arbitrate a dispute concerning an inheritance (Luke 12:13–14). How many modern priests would treat such a question as alien to their office?

Certainly some of the problems of the moral teaching office will be removed if it is recognized that the Church produces adult Christians with responsible moral judgment. These adults do not need control, we trust; if they do need it, the Church has failed to a degree which moral control will not repair.

[13] Rudolf Schnackenburg, *The Moral Teaching of the New Testament,* translated from German (New York: Herder and Herder, 1965) 90–109.

There are a number of ways in which the Church can influence the moral judgment of the faithful other than detailed directions; but moral instruction has largely abandoned these other ways. What these other ways are can be learned by reading the New Testament. Reading the New Testament may also plant in our minds the suspicion that detailed moral directions show little confidence in the individual conscience and not much confidence in the power of the gospel.

There are at least some extreme limits of the teaching office of the Church which seem obvious. The teaching office is not empowered to control either the world of learning or the world of morality. The teaching office is not commissioned to tell people what to do, but to make it possible for people to decide what to do. That people will err must be expected, and, when they do err, the temptation to exercise control is very attractive. The damage which error works must be weighed against the damage which control works; and this measurement has not been made often enough. The image of the omnicompetent teacher will be shattered because it is unreal; and when the image is shattered, the danger of the loss of faith arises. The Church does best what Jesus Christ empowered it to do, and he did not empower the Church to be every man's schoolmaster and every man's conscience. By attempting the impossible the officers of the Church sometimes lose the possible.

Must we not recall that the mission of the Church is not the exclusive responsibility of her officers, but a responsibility shared by the whole Church? In the area of teaching it is the mission of the Christian scholar to serve the Church by his learning. In the area of morality it is the mission of every Christian to translate the moral revolution of the gospel into his own situation in life. We do not understand the reality of the teaching office if we think the office is the sole responsibility of official teachers. Official teachers teach in a way in which those who are not officers cannot; but the officers cannot teach

as officers unless their work is integrated with the teaching—
and this is the proper word—of other members of the Church.
Integration here does not mean control, but cooperation and
mutual encouragement. Official teachers of the Church know
that they too must exhibit the virtue which is basic for every
good teacher; this virtue is the ability to learn from anyone.
In 1859 Newman wrote an article entitled, "On Consulting the
Faithful in Matters of Doctrine." Recently reprinted,[13a] the
title of the article evoked as much surprise now as when the
article first appeared. The surprise that anyone would speak
of consulting the faithful is a clear indication that the popular
idea of the teaching office needs revision.

[13a] New York: Sheed and Ward, 1962.

11. The Organization

WHEN, IN 1956, WILLIAM H. WHYTE, JR., published an ingenious book called *The Organization Man*,[14] a number of clergymen who read this sociological and psychological analysis of the managerial class of modern corporations experienced an uneasy feeling of *déja vu*. The book seemed to bring out many things which they already knew from their familiarity with the ecclesiastical community. Sooner or later they were appalled to recognize in the book a caricature of religious obedience, but a caricature so close to the truth that it was uncomfortable. Consider some of the titles and subtitles in the book: belongingness; togetherness; a generation of bureaucrats; the tests of conformity; the fight against genius; love that system; society as hero. The Organization demands a type of obedience, submission, and conformity which only the Church can demand. The feeling of uneasiness grows with the question whether even the Church can demand it.

Mr. Whyte's charge against the modern corporation is that, with the full consent and cooperation of those whom it devours, The Organization guarantees security at the price of depersonalization. The Organization takes over more and more of the personal decision of those to whom it offers promotion until they are reduced to a type in which the individual does all he can to avoid what would make him stand out from the type as an individual. It is social pressure and not explicit

[14] *The Organization Man* (New York: Simon and Schuster, 1956).

written Organization policy that dictates even the type of clothing the man wears, the type of home he buys or builds, the type of automobile he owns, the types of recreation which are proper and permitted. Mr. Whyte wryly observes that the Corporation does not yet select the wives of its officers, but it has created a type to which the wife must conform. Mr. Whyte did not intend to write a satire on a theology of salvation, but he succeeded in writing it. His book should be required reading for all who have any dealings with Church authority, whether they bear authority or are subject to it.

Our question is whether the Church should become The Organization or whether the Church can adopt the techniques of The Organization. Precisely, is the end of the Church served if the Church adopts belongingness, togetherness, bureaucracy, conformity, system, the fight against genius, and the idolization of society? My thesis, which may be no more than a restatement of previous pages, is that, to the extent that one thinks of the Church as The Organization, one ceases to think of it as the Church; that the techniques of The Organization are not only useless for the end of the Church, but they are positively opposed to that end. The Church has an organization; it is not an organization. The Church is the body of Christ in which the Spirit dwells. Yet it seems worth while to consider the techniques of The Organization because these techniques are undoubtedly tempting to Church officers.

The key word of all those I have mentioned is conformity. Conformity is by definition not obedience; it is both more than obedience and less than obedience. Conformity is more than obedience because it extends over a far wider area of thought and action than obedience touches; conformity is less than obedience because conformity is a less dignified human action. Obedience does not demand depersonalization, and it should be noticed that the denial of self, the Gospel phrase (Matthew 16:24; Mark 8:34; Luke 9:23), or the surrender of self, so

often mentioned in ascetical literature, is not depersonalization.
The self which is surrendered or denied is the Pauline "old
man" (Romans 6:6; Ephesians 4:22; Colossians 3:9). The
old man dies that the new man may emerge who is alive to
God in Christ Jesus (Romans 6:11). The New Testament
knows no conformity except conformity to Christ; and to
think of Jesus Christ as a prototype of conformity—a kind of
original Man in the Grey Flannel Suit—is not only irreverent,
but it approaches blasphemy.

In Mr. Whyte's world, The Organization usurps the place
of the body of Christ and the Spirit. The Organization transforms its members the only way an organization can transform
them; for The Organization is impersonal and it transforms
men into its own image and likeness. The Organization seeks
that conformity which can be supervised, which is external
conformity in speech, dress, and deportment. To what extent
conformity reaches the inner man is open to question; Mr.
Whyte believes that it reaches very deeply and that the secret
nonconformist will sooner or later betray himself and suffer
the damnation of the Organization *Heilsgeschichte.* This is not
loss of soul, but loss of status. If the Organization Man is to
speak as he ought, he must develop the habit of thinking nothing but what The Organization thinks. If the Organization
Man is to be the perfect instrument of Organization policy, he
must be so deeply identified with the policy that a doubt never
crosses his mind. In every situation of major or minor importance, in private life or in public, in personal affairs or in
business affairs, his first and last question must be: "What does
the Organization want me to do?" And there will always be an
answer. The Organization is what, in the preceding chapter,
I said the Church is not—an omnicompetent authority which
is never without an answer and never without directions.

I have said that The Organization usurps the place of the
Church; I ask now whether the only thing wrong with The

Organization's domination over its members is that it is The
Organization and not the Church which dominates. No one,
I trust, believes that the Church can become the demonic Organization described by Mr. Whyte. However, when one goes
over each of the items by which The Organization acquires
such complete control over its members that it destroys them,
one finds that each step has its defenders within the Church
and has been practiced within the Church. It is the tactics
themselves which need discussion, not the identity of the agent
who employs the tactics. We cannot assume that these are good
tactics which have fallen into the wrong hands. Used by The
Organization, these tactics destroy; it is a doubtful assumption
that the same tactics, used by the Church, will build up the
body of Christ.

Conformity has long been a mark of those organizations
within the Church which are called religious communities.
These communities wear a distinctive and uniform habit, follow one rule for all members, engage in the same ministries,
and live in houses built according to a pattern (I can rarely
tell Jesuits simply by looking at them, but I have rarely failed
to recognize a Jesuit house by looking at it). Most of these
communities even abandon the baptismal and family names of
candidates as an external sign that the old man has perished;
it should be noticed that a new name is conferred which signifies that a new person has emerged. It is a witness to the
genius of Christianity that these organizations do not succeed
in suppressing individual personality. My own Society has
fewer of these external signs of conformity than most other
communities; but the Society has a reputation for producing
men who run to type. One needs only some acquaintance with
the Society to realize that this reputation is quite unmerited;
I have to add that the reputation is unmerited in spite of a
constant and sturdy tradition within the Society which tends
to produce a type. Were members of religious communities

motivated as are Organization Men, conformity would long
since have been achieved as it is in The Organization.

Religious communities, however, are specialized minority
groups within the Church. The communities are approved by
the Holy See as representatives of the Christian life; but the
Christian life does not consist in this system of conformity and
discipline practiced in religious communities. The Church ap-
proves religious rules as means to an end, not as ends in themselves; and the Church teaches that those who do not live
under religious rule and discipline are under no disadvantage
in the pursuit of their Christian fulfilment. Approval of the
religious life does not signify disapproval of the secular life in
which the vast majority of Christians live. This life needs no
explicit approval from the Church.

Setting aside, then, the religious life as a specialized manner
of life, we can say that conformity and system are two items
in our list which have no basis in the New Testament; yet the
presence of conformity and system in the Church needs no
demonstration. Conformity and system are spurious imitations
of Christian obedience. Yet conformity and system have a
strange attraction because they are easier than obedience from
the superior's point of view and, by a quaint coincidence, from
the subject's point of view as well. System removes the necessity of thought and of dealing with individual situations as
individual. In a well organized, systematic routine a prefab-
ricated decision can be found in the files for every conceivable
situation except a major crisis. It is just where decision is most
necessary that the system provides no decision. It will be urged
that I present an impossible ideal which ecclesiastical superiors
cannot achieve because they do not have the time to deal
personally with all their subjects. But I do not imply that the
number of genuinely individual situations is great. I suggest
that ecclesiastical superiors do not have the time for this because the system and tradition have imposed upon them a great

number of duties which they ought not to have. I suggest further that a kind of creeping authoritarianism has reduced the number of decisions which could well be left to the individual subject and imposed them upon the superior. One is sometimes appalled at the amount of time which is consumed by both superiors and subjects in obtaining permission to do something which is perfectly moral and fully in harmony with the rules and spirit of the organization and which disturbs neither the work of the organization nor other members. Conformity is easily seen, and conformity permits the management of large numbers in groups because the members become interchangeable parts. Conformity reduces the person to a thing; and The Organization controls things much better than it controls persons. The Church in her law renounces jurisdiction over what is called "the internal forum," the area of conscience. "The external forum" covers those cases which are subject to a legal process. In practice, unfortunately, the distinction is not perfect. There is a large twilight zone of words and actions which are not subject to legal process, but which are external. Because these words and actions are external, authority is interested in them.

Ought authority to be interested in all external conduct? Authority and obedience by the constitution of the Church are concerned with those words and actions which belong to the mission of the Church. If authority is intent on its objective, it finds the mission of the Church a full-time occupation. Authority will do well if it achieves harmony and cooperation among the members and if it prevents false starts and duplication of effort; these are unattained objectives for which authority can legitimately begin to strive at any time—now, for instance. The Constitution on the Church of the Second Vatican Council mentions a number of responsibilities which lie upon bishops, and these can, with proper adaptations, be ap-

plied to other ecclesiastical superiors.[15] These include the proclamation of the gospel, the promotion of unity of faith, love
and discipline, the promotion of every activity that is of interest to the whole Church, the supplying of workers and of
spiritual and material aid, the sponsoring of cooperation
among the faithful, the provision of aid to more needy dioceses
and—not least important—the selection of worthy candidates
for the episcopacy. The interests which yield when a superior's
time must be consumed with the granting of routine permis-
sions are not trivial. Should these primary interests be the
concern of authority, authority will have neither the time nor
the resources to supervise those words and actions which belong
to the personal decision of the members of the Church as a
part of the personal Christian fulfilment of each member.
Church authority can and ought to ignore most of what the
members of the Church do; system and conformity in theory
ignore nothing. The purpose of system and conformity is not
the accomplishment of a mission, but complete control over all
the persons who are involved in the system. Nothing is left to
the Holy Spirit who is presumed to operate exclusively through
and within the system. The objective of control is the transformation of persons into a type. In a system of conformity
there is nothing, including one's thoughts and daydreams,
which is not the concern of the governing body. No personal
growth and no personal achievement are envisaged; The Organization is all and does all.

Is this the Church? Of all the secular forms which the
Church can take, this form is perhaps the most insidious. A
number of New Testament texts can be cited which, taken by
themselves, support the organizational ideal of conformity.
These texts have to be taken by themselves, because one has
to forget that The Organization is a human society with human

[15] Butler and Baum, *op. cit.*, chapter III, #23.

ends to be achieved by human means. In The Organization there is no authority beyond the official hierarchy; in the Church there is the Spirit. The Organization does not achieve its end through the personal fulfilment of each of its members; this is exactly the way in which the Church achieves its end. The Organization uses its techniques because it needs total control over its members, or thinks it does. Church authority does not need total control for the end of the Church; and the New Testament expressly forbids total control when it likens the officers of the Church to children and lackeys. Where total control is forbidden, there is no need of conformity. Conformity is not unity, and all who deal with human beings know it. Conformity is a superficial species of unity which can be imposed for a limited purpose, as in an army or an athletic team. The Organization has made conformity a way of life; Mr. Whyte and others think that it will prove to be a way of death. Of all the substitutes for genuine leadership, conformity and system are the most shoddy and the least respectful of basic human dignity.

We turn to bureaucracy. The Church has grown to vast proportions and engages in a complex variety of activities. The question can be raised whether the Church could not divest herself of some of these activities, but this question, while it ought to be raised, cannot be answered here. In order to manage this immense machinery, bureaucracy is the necessary instrument. But bureaucracy is an instrument of authority; bureaucracy is not authority. If we consider authority as only one of the functions of the Church, as we have done, we must consider bureaucracy as one of the functions of authority, and not the primary function. The suggestion has recently been made that many bureaucratic offices in the Church would be better filled by laymen than by priests. I see no assurance that this change would prevent the rise of a lay bureaucracy, and I have no reason for preferring either a clerical bureaucracy or a lay bureaucracy. I have referred to the obvious danger that administrators may view the ministries of the Church not only from the outside, but also as of lower dignity and importance than the work of administration. When this view arises, the Church takes on some of the features of The Organization. It is surely not without interest that Max Weber included the Roman Catholic Church since the thirteenth century in his list of "distinctly developed and quantitatively large bureaucracies."[16] The other examples, for those who wish to pursue the topic further, are Egypt of the New Kingdom, the later Roman Principate (especially under Diocletian), China, the modern European states, and the large modern capitalist corporation.

Belongingness and togetherness in The Organization are spurious imitations of Christian love. These unhappy words and the phenomena which they designate are the very opposite of the intense interpersonal union which Christian love achieves. Like conformity, they are merely external. Belongingness and togetherness are means of bringing together depersonalized shells of men who have no genuine interest in each other except as fellow components of The Organization which guarantees their common security so long as they hold it in common. Theirs is the community of shipwrecked men on a raft, the community of a desire to survive. Such a community does not form brotherhood, although it can create a very high degree of discipline and cooperation. The community of survival does not demand that men cease to be selfish; it simply makes selfishness a community affair. The Organization, like the raft, is the common security; and part of the price of accepting the security is accepting all those who are engaged in the activities of The Organization, and just as far as

[16] H. H. Gerth and C. Wright Mills, editors, *From Max Weber* (New York: Oxford University Press, 1958), 204. The entire essay ("Bureaucracy," 196–244) is well worth reflective reading.

they are engaged. One difference between The Organization
and the community of the raft is that the community of the
raft hopes to return to normal living. The Organization Man
gives nothing of himself because he really has no self to give.
That people mistake "togetherness" for Christian love seems
so evident that it needs no demonstration; and kindness forbids
the citation of concrete examples except the remark of an educational administrator in a religious community. The remark
was that he was not interested in the personal achievements
of the members of his faculty, but only in how they fit into the
organization. The Church has not become The Organization
and it will not; but the same *charisma* does not operate to protect Catholic colleges and universities.

The phrase, "the fight against genius," recalls the number
of distinguished Catholic scholars in our generation who have
been harassed and in some instances reduced to temporary or
permanent silence. These men have never been explicitly
charged with any deviation from sound doctrine; if they were
secretly charged, they had no opportunity to explain their
position or to defend it. One simply does not know the processes involved because the processes are not disclosed. These
men have exhibited a submissive obedience which ought to
satisfy the most ardent defender of authority. They are men
whose work for the Church will be long remembered and used;
and it is some comfort to know that their memory will live in
the Church when those who did not cooperate with their work
—to put it mildly—will be remembered, if at all, only for
their connection with these scholars. The opponents of learning will have the position in history occupied by Etienne
Tempier, and for those who are not well informed on medieval
Paris, Etienne Tempier was the Archbishop of Paris who
condemned the writings of Thomas Aquinas in 1277. This
immortality is of such a dubious character that one should
hesitate before one risks sharing it. The Church has many more

like Tempier than it has like Aquinas, and, were it not for men like Tempier, there would be more like Aquinas.

Genius is repellent to the Organization bureaucrat because he cannot control it. I say the Organization bureaucrat because I do not wish to make the unfair mistake of typing ecclesiastical administrators. It must be said that no Catholic is known who achieved success in scholarship or in anything else without the sympathy and the active cooperation of Church officers. The long series of men who have achieved notably in the Church is the most solid demonstration that the Church is not The Organization. But the Church has Organization Men, and they do harm. There is no way of computing the number of those who did not achieve the work of which they were capable because they were denied the sympathy and the active cooperation of Church officers. The Organization Men do harm in these instances precisely because they wish a type of control which no man, whatever his office may be, should have over another. It is a common form of vanity and arrogance to refuse to recognize the potentialities and achievements of others which are lacking in one's self. This ill becomes a churchman as poorly as disobedience and insubmissiveness become the subjects of the churchman. Gratitude and not fear is the proper response when one realizes the presence of unusual talent combined with an active desire to use the talent. It seems stupid to add that the possessor of the talent is an excellent judge of how to develop and employ the talent. At the same time, the fight against genius shows that the remark is necessary, even if it is stupid.

The last of the phrases which I have selected for comment is "society as hero." The attitude indicated by this phrase is also an insidious but spurious imitation of something in the Church. When one thinks of the Church as the body of Christ and the temple of the Spirit, and when one contemplates the reality of the Church in the past and in the present, one could grow as lyrical as St. Paul if one had Paul's gift of language. Experience of the Church makes apologetic arguments for her divine mission and her divine reality absolutely superficial. In the Church one encounters the living presence of Jesus Christ in the world. And it is just this which separates the Church from The Organization. The Organization is a hollow shell, like the people whom it transforms. In The Organization one may experience efficiency to a marvelous degree, excellent management on all levels, equity and fairness to the personnel, perfect integration of diverse operations—all with mechanical perfection. One understands why The Organization Man abdicates his personality to identify himself with something so big and so successful. The Organization is a splendid, inhuman operation, and it pays well.

There is a subtle difference between faith in the Church as the body of Christ and veneration of The Organization as hero. In the one instance, one denies one's self to put on Christ; in the other, one depersonalizes one's self in order to become The Organization Man. The one brings an increased awareness of personal responsibility; the other diminishes personal responsibility to the vanishing point. The one invites to the following of Jesus and the carrying of the cross; the other promises security in committing one's life to the decisions of others and an infallible routine. What it comes to is this: in the Church one may seek and find benefits and rewards of a purely human and secular character.[17] One puts one's faith in a system rather than in the Incarnate Word, in routine rather than in the Spirit. One depends on the human structure more than on the reality of the Church as the living Christ.

The Organization represents power, not the Spirit, and power is the besetting temptation of Church authority. It is

[17] Some of the "in-built problems" of promotion in the ecclesiastical career are treated by Joseph A. Fichter, *Religion as an Occupation* 171–175.

not abnormal or surprising that power should be the most
seductive temptation for men who have renounced the pros-
pect of wealth and the pleasures of love. The possession of
power assures one of rare and distinctive status in one's community; by secular standards it assures the highest status. No
one is so surely in the Church, so surely identified with the
Church as those who hold power in the Church; they can
claim a recognition which no one else can claim. Power is the
most ascetic and spiritual of vices; it is also the most diabolical.
Power demands a renunciation strangely like the renunciation
which Jesus imposes on his followers. Men who are devoted to
the acquisition and the retention of secular power, it is well
known, have neither the time for grosser vices nor interest in
them. The austerity of the private lives of powerful men often
differs little in its external features from the life of the monk.
These men are capable of sustained work which would break
a man of less intense dedication. This is the price which they
gladly pay for power and its accompanying status; the reward
in their valuation exceeds the price. Evidently the Christian
life consists in more than austerity and dedication.

Power, more than other things, recommends itself as a
means for a noble end. Most men who have achieved great
power were convinced, at least at the beginning of their career,
that they sought power only for the good they could not accomplish without power. There is no reason to doubt the sin-
cerity of their conviction. Once they became entrenched in
power, the altruism of their motives becomes obscured. The
renunciation of power and status is far more painful than any
renunciation of personal pleasure, or leisure, or convenience
incidental to the retention of power. At the very least, they are
compelled to retain power because of the fearful prospects
which await them if they lose it. Power in the Church, even
more than secular power, can appear as the sole means by
which great good can be accomplished. It is not always easy to

discern that when one puts one's faith in power, one effectively gives up one's faith in the Spirit. One loses sight of the truth that the Church accomplishes nothing except what the members of the Church freely wish that the Church accomplish. The Church has no power other than the life of Christ in its members; and this life is not subject to compulsion.

12. The Prophetic Office

THE PROPHETIC OFFICE is one of the most distinctive features of the religion of Israel as it is described in the Old Testament. The prophet (thought by many modern scholars to be "one called" [to speak]) was a charismatic person whose *charisma* was the word of God. In the name of the God of Israel the prophet uttered threats and warnings or promises and blessings. He denounced sin and crime both in individual persons and in the community in general. His denunciations were not restricted to religion in the strictest sense of the term; they touched the entire order of morality and even public policy. The prophet interpreted the will of God as it was revealed in Israelite traditions and applied the will of God to existing situations.

The prophet was not an official of the Israelite community. We know of no institutional appointment by which the prophet received his commission to be the spokesman of God. The few prophets, like Amos, Isaiah, and Jeremiah who spoke of their commission, attributed the commission to a mystical experience and not to human authority. The prophetic commission could not be handed on by the prophet to another; only God could call a prophet. When the prophets encountered the officials of the Israelite community, whether secular or religious, the relations between the prophet and officials were usually hostile. The prophets did not exclude kings and priests from their denunciations; indeed, the responsible position of such officers increased their share in the national guilt. The failure of Israel to live under the will of God was, in the first place, a failure of national leadership, both religious and political. The prophets stood outside the political and hierarchical structure of the Israelite community, and it is extremely difficult to define their position in the community in terms intelligible to us.

"Prophets" appear in the New Testament also, we have noticed, but their function is much more obscure. New Testament prophets are mentioned rarely, and nothing suggests that they served the apostolic Church as the Old Testament prophets served Israel. Furthermore, while the New Testament prophets are not clearly officers of the Church in the technical sense, they do not stand entirely outside the structure of Church authority. Prophecy is one of the gifts enumerated in the lists we have noticed; these gifts lie under the supervision of Church officers. We know too little about the New Testament prophets to find in their function an answer to the question whether the prophetic office exists in the modern Church and where the prophetic office is located.

That the prophetic office does exist in the modern Church is really questioned by no one.[18] Jesus cannot be called simply a prophet; he falls into no category. But Jesus exhibits all the features of the prophet. He spoke the word of God; he uttered denunciations and promises; and he stood outside the hierarchical structure of Judaism. If the Church does not exercise the prophetic office, she fails to carry on a part of the mission of Jesus. But a question arises here which is less easily answered than it is for the Old Testament prophets. The mission of the prophets was directed principally to the community of Israel of which the prophets were members, and secondarily to the non-Israelite nations. The prophetic mission of the Church to the world is easily seen in her proclamation of the

[18] Butler and Baum, *op. cit.*, chapter II, #12.

gospel to the world. Is there a prophetic office within the Church? And, if there is, who are the bearers of the office?

We have seen that the authority which Jesus instituted in his Church is entirely original; it is not derived from Judaism or from existing political forms. The prophetic office belongs to the whole Church, as do all the functions of the Church; and authority will play its proper part in prophecy without monopolizing the function. But prophecy within the Church must be an address of members of the Church to other members or to the whole Church. Is prophecy within the Church the function of authority? To this question no answer but the affirmative is possible. If authority never addresses the members of the Church with a prophetic voice, authority fails in its duty. But is prophecy also the function of other members of the Church? Is prophecy in the Church official and hierarchical in the sense that the *charisma* of prophecy comes only to those who are appointed to office? Is there a prophecy which is not uttered by authority, but is uttered to authority?

The nature of prophecy and the nature of the Church indicate that prophecy belongs to the whole Church, not to Church officers alone, and that the officers can hear prophecy as well as speak it. If prophecy were an exclusively hierarchical function, it would lose something which it exhibits in the Old Testament and in Jesus, and this is its detachment from the official structure. It is precisely this detachment which gives prophecy the freedom it needs. The structure of the Church, which is fraternal and not autocratic, gives ample room for members who are not officers to speak to the officers. If the members of the Church cannot speak with prophetic authority, it would mean that the Spirit does not dwell in the whole Church, but only in the hierarchy.

The history of the Church attests both the need of prophecy within the Church and its existence. Prophecy within the Church is a remedy against corruption on all levels. There are

times when the officers of the Church fail to speak as they
ought; those who utter the authentic voice of the Church in
such moments are prophets. There are times when the hierarchy itself needs to be redeemed from corruption; those who
rebuke it are prophets. Prophecy in such times of need can
be either speech or action. Prophecy is found in any class or
level in the Church; and it is not limited to men. Prophecy is
recognized as the operation of the Spirit by the fact that it is
for the good of the Church and that it comes from no official
direction. Certainly among prophets one would have to include most of the founders of religious communities—in particular, Francis of Assisi—who was not celebrated as a
speaker. Ignatius Loyola, whose name has become identified
with obedience, spent a short time in the prison of the Inquisi-
tion and emerged unrepentant and unbowed. Catherine of
Siena clearly spoke for the Church when its officers seemed
incapable of doing so. Thomas More had almost no episcopal
support in his stand. There is no doubt that the Church has
had prophets, and no doubt that she has them still. And it
must be noticed that those who merit the title have had, in
almost every instance, a hostile encounter with some of the
officers of the Church. Here one of the characteristics of Old
Testament prophecy endures.

Prophecy, as a work of the Spirit, is a component of Church
authority; and here we see clearly that authority in the Church
cannot be identified totally with the official hierarchy of the
Church. Whatever distinction one cares to make on the word
"authority," the authority of the prophet can be denied only by
denying the presence and the power of the Spirit. The function
of the prophet is certainly not to administer, not to hold office,
not to exercise that type of leadership which the officer is
entitled and obliged to exercise. But if he is a prophet, he
speaks with authority; and authority in the Church has to be
conceived in terms which leave room for the prophetic spokes-

man. For the Spirit is the basis of the authority both of the officers of the Church and of prophets; and the Spirit does not inhibit his own power in one channel when he speaks or acts through another channel. Prophecy is the only agency of the Spirit through which any control is exercised over the officers themselves and through which those defects and sins can be corrected which it cannot be assumed the officers themselves will correct. There is no room for prophecy in the Church if the hierarchical officers of the Church always rise to their duty. The history of the Church up to this point does not permit this hypothesis.

However, there are uncertainties in the prophetic mission. There are true prophets and false prophets. How does one distinguish the true from the false? More vitally, how does the prophet himself know that he has a genuine call and that he is speaking under the inspiration of the Spirit? The Old Testament furnishes us with no infallible answer to the first question other than this, that the true prophet is recognized by the harmony of what he says with the traditional faith of Israel. For the prophet himself, the Old Testament gives no assurance except the assurance which is based on personal insight and conviction. Similar principles should be valid for the Church. The true prophet is recognized not only by the criterion of concord with the traditional faith of the Church, but also by whether his message supports unity in faith and in love, or whether it makes for disunity. The prophetic mission is undertaken with risk, for, even if the prophet has a genuine call, he may delude himself in the course of his mission. The officers of the Church have no uncertainty about their call because they are authentic officers by appointment. But they are no better protected than the prophet against self-deception in the execution of their mission.

Because there are false prophets, it does not follow that there are no true prophets. Because prophets and their listeners can be deceived, it does not follow that they are always deceived. To run from the risk of prophecy to the specious security of organization may be to run from the Holy Spirit. To ask how one knows that a prophet is a true prophet poses a question no more difficult than the question of how one knows that an officer of the Church speaks beyond the competence of his authority. This can happen, and it can be discerned. Prophecy, it must be admitted, occurs when other channels have become clouded and thinking is confused. When a crisis has arisen which demands prophetic utterance, the crisis makes it more difficult to recognize the prophet. Is the difficulty due to a lack of clarity in the prophet's words or to the confused thinking of those whom the prophet addresses? The very clarity of the prophet's message can make it hard for those whose spiritual vision has become dulled to perceive the truth of the message. We have no trouble seeing this in the prophecy of the Old Testament; it is something altogether different when we are forced to ask ourselves whether a prophet is speaking to us about ourselves.

We need not think of the prophet as addressing the whole Church from some international podium, or a whole continent or nation. The prophet may speak in a single diocese or in a single parish. What is important is to recognize that there is no order, rank, sex or even age which is excluded from prophecy. The legend which tells that Ambrose was elected bishop because a child cried out, "Ambrose is bishop," attests the belief of the Church that even children can utter prophecy, although it must be admitted that this is extremely rare. But it shows that we have no business determining antecedently who shall and who shall not be the channels of prophecy. Prophecy does not demand learning, or wisdom, or experience. Prophecy is not a career. When prophecy is needed, the Spirit acts; and I believe the Spirit calls to prophecy more frequently than we recognize. I believe that the Spirit calls many in vain. Because of timidity or social pressure those whom the Spirit calls do not say what they know the Spirit moves them to say; and the Church is so much the loser. I reserve for later discussion the suppression of prophecy by the officers of the Church.

There can be no doubt that the usual hostility which we see existing in the Old Testament between prophets and the officers of Israel is continued in the history of the Church. If one ranks Joan of Arc as a prophet—and it seems one must—one must observe that the officers of the Church took a long time to reverse the verdict of an ecclesiastical court which was suborned. If one ranks Savonarola as a prophet, one again observes a long delay in doing him justice; and I believe he deserves the title. Savonarola is a good example because he illustrates the human limitations of the prophet and some degree of delusion mixed with his message, as well as the use of means inept for his end. I do not know why things like this should make a prophet illegitimate when they do not deprive the officer of the Church of his jurisdiction. At least no historian has questioned Savonarola's honesty, which is more than one can say of the prelates with whom he was engaged.

Is it a part of the demonic in man that prophecy must usually meet Church authority on the level of hostility? In the story of prophets the fault is scarcely ever all on one side; the story of prophets in this does not differ from the story of almost every transaction in which human beings are involved. But the ugly fact is that Church authority can suppress prophets, and prophets cannot suppress Church authority. All a prophet can do is incite a revolution, and, if he does this, he imperils the integrity of his prophetic mission. Why does suppression seem to be the normal and instinctive reaction of authority to prophecy? It surely is something deeper than the mere fact that prophets often rebuke authority; the Church is not yet that poor in men who can accept criticism.

I suggest that authority is suspicious of prophets because

a prophet, as the spokesman inspired by the Spirit, by definition cannot be controlled. I have urged earlier that control is something which Church authority has no right to seek or to exercise; prophecy is an excellent illustration of this. For if the prophet speaks by the Spirit, he speaks with authority; and at once the threat of multiple seats of authority arises. The New Testament explains clearly that this is no real threat, for authority belongs to the Church, not solely to her officers. There are different gifts, but one and the same Spirit. The prophet performs a function which the officers, as officers, cannot perform; the officers, because they cannot perform the function, can come to think that no one should perform it. The prophet speaks with an assurance which is not given him by Church authority; he may be as obedient and submissive as one could desire, but so long as he is a prophet, he cannot be managed. The prophet remains outside the structure of official authority. The question which officers have been known to ask is whether there is anything in the Church which should be outside this structure. So Savonarola and a few of his associates were burned at the stake from which they had been hung, and authority was saved. I have never heard anyone say that the blunder of the Church between 1517 and 1521 was that the officers of the Church did not do to Luther what was done to John Huss at Constance. Luther certainly expected it and took means to protect himself. Had the officers taken this vigorous action, it would again have saved authority in a crisis by postponing the crisis. When authority feels itself endangered by a prophet, authority has not always examined the prophet too closely to see whether he was genuine or not. If one wants to be a prophet, one must think of oneself as expendable.

The English have a word which describes a whole complex system; they speak of the Establishment. By this term they mean a small closely knit and interrelated group of families who form the upper ruling class of the country, who control the external and internal politics, most of the money, and most of the thinking. The Establishment works within a system of British liberties which have long been the model of democratic society; but it works, by which I mean that the Establishment remains the Establishment. Accepting the word without becoming involved in any discussion of how much the idea corresponds to reality, let us ask whether the relations of prophecy to Church authority are not often relations with an Establishment rather than with an authority.

We have left no doubt, I hope, that Jesus Christ founded a Church with authority and with officers. We should not have to prove that Jesus did not found an Establishment. As Church authority is described in the New Testament, a prophet could not possibly threaten it. Should authority fail of its duty because of human weakness, or plain lack of thought, or even from bad will, the authority which knows that it is the lackey and the slave of the Church will recognize that in prophecy authority has one of its strongest supports. Prophecy will keep Church authority what it ought to be. When we ask who will control prophets, why do we never ask who will control the controllers? But prophecy is a threat to an Establishment, and a very serious threat. Church authority is hostile to prophecy to the degree that Church authority has become an Establishment. The idea of an Establishment is so foreign to the New Testament idea of Church authority that it is one of the first things a prophet would mention. The Church is no one's vested interest, no one's financial or social security, no one's fief, no one's career, and certainly no one's seat of power and status symbol. An Establishment or a ruling class, if I read Galatians 3:28 and Colossians 3:11 correctly, is totally alien to the constitution of the Church.

In the preceding chapter I used another somewhat odious term: The Organization. The prophet is also hostile to the

Church as The Organization. The Organization, wherever it appears, survives by standardizing a routine. To a certain extent The Organization canonizes mediocrity because there is more mediocrity available than there is anything else. The prophet is a herald of change; if he has no change to recommend, he has nothing to say. If he is a true prophet, the changes he demands will not be minor, and they will make a great many people uncomfortable. It is prophecy, above all, which keeps the Church from becoming The Organization. The prophet will not let the Church stagnate in comfort and indolence. Just when we think that we are doing all we ought as well as we ought, a prophet arises to point out some vital area in which we are doing nothing or to tell us that much of what we are doing is not the work of the Church. The officers of the Church are by no means the only members of the Church who are unfriendly to prophets. We all dislike them.

The prophets, like the poor, are always with us. Were it not for their failure to heed their call and for suppression, they would be with us in larger numbers. The suppression of prophecy by Church officers is too important a question for the imputation of motives. The fact is that, when an organization has become rigid, it is extremely difficult to tolerate deviations of any kind. We protect a rigid organization because we have never learned to manage a flexible organization. We have identified the organization with the Church so closely that anything which seems to point out a defect in the organization or to suggest a modification in structure or administration is taken as an attack on the Church itself. The prophet is outside the official structure, and therefore we think that he is outside the Church; but the two are not the same thing at all. We shall escape this error, I think, if we remember that the prophet is a part of Church authority and if we learn that, in order to have true prophets, we must put up with some false prophets. Church officers have not always shown that they can surely tell one from the other.

The prophetic call is a great and fearful thing. The one who receives it has a great responsibility, and this he has in common with the officers of the Church; but he can evade his responsibility more easily than they can. His friends will all assure him that he should not rock the boat, wash dirty linen in public, foul his own nest, or do any of the things which these homely old saws call imprudence. I suppose Amos must have known people who gave him this advice. With the prophetic call there comes an awareness of the danger of self-deception, of abuse of the *charisma*. The prophet recognizes that he who receives a rare capacity for serving the Church has also received a rare capacity for doing harm to the Church, and here, too, he will recognize that he has something in common with her officers. And this is the most fearful part of his mission, compared to which any risk of personal suffering is trivial.

13. The Tension between Authority and Freedom

IN EVERY SOCIETY there is tension between freedom and authority, a tension which varies with the strength of the two poles. This tension exists in the Church too, and it seems worth saying that the tension ought to exist. In a vital organism tension is a sign of life, and the absence of tension is a sign of death. The metaphor is also valid of a society. Were there no tension between freedom and authority in the Church, it would mean that either freedom or authority had vanished; and neither the defenders of authority nor the defenders of freedom, however devoted they may be to their causes, can really hope for the disappearance of the opposite pole. But not every species of tension is healthy, and it will reward us to consider what the tension ought and ought not to be.

Let the preliminary remark be made that freedom is not given by one man to another. Man is free by nature, not by grant. One man cannot give another freedom; he can only restrain freedom or remove restraint. The ultimate basis for the restraint of freedom is the freedom of the person who restrains, for there is no valid reason for restraining the freedom of one except to preserve the freedom of others. Nor does the abstract freedom which is every man's by his nature add up to an equal portion of freedom for each. In existing reality some need more freedom than others, and the degree of freedom which one has is measured by the degree of responsibility which he has. Parents have greater freedom than children. To meet our problem in this study, those who bear authority in the Church need and have more freedom than those who do not bear authority. What is important is to remember that the freedom neither of those in authority nor of those under authority is granted by the other party.

If this principle is retained, it will become clear that the ultimate and most effective protection of authority is not power, but freedom. For authority is freedom and, in this sense, authority is power. But authority cannot endure unless it defends freedom, which means the freedom of those under authority as well as those who bear authority. Privation of the freedom of another deprives me of my own freedom; for I have by the privation put myself under the compulsion of defending a position which I had no right to take. I have rendered my authority insecure by abusing it; and I am now hampered in its use. When authority recognizes the freedom of those whom it governs, it has done all it can to secure its own freedom. And authority does not recognize freedom unless it recognizes that freedom in anyone is power. When authority recognizes freedom, authority has that unique security which comes from the free consent of those who are subject to authority; their power is merged with its own.

The recognition of freedom does not remove tension between authority and freedom, but it sustains a healthy tension. For authority and freedom (actually they are both species of freedom) are extremely active principles, each principle tending to realize its own fullness. Hannah Arendt asserts that freedom is not an attribute of the will but of action.[19] Man proves his freedom by what he does rather than by what he wishes, and that freedom which does not issue in action is

[19] *Between Past and Future,* 143–171.

regarded as purely theoretical at best, as illusory non-freedom
at worst. Without restraint, freedom and authority tend to destroy each other. This is the nature of the two principles. The
paradox is not resolved by allowing one principle to destroy
the other any more than one would choose to get along with
either fire or water, but by allowing each principle to exercise
that restraint upon the other which no other principle can
exercise. There is no restraint of freedom except authority,
and no restraint of authority except freedom. If the principles
are to operate as they ought, there must be mutual recognition
and respect. This is healthy tension which cannot be removed
from society, whether it be the Church or any other society.
The presence of this tension is a sign of strength, not of
weakness.

Both authority and freedom are vested in men, not angels.
The failure of men to act at all times acording to their intelligent judgment and sincere good will creates tensions which
are not healthy. Both authority and freedom always feel dis-
satisfied with anything less than total lack of restraint. Where
the point of restraint is to be placed is a matter of judgment.
It is a vice both of authority and of those who seek freedom
to think that this is a unilateral decision. A unilateral decision
made by either side will infallibly be wrong. Mutual recognition and respect include a readiness to accept mistakes as
one hopes to have one's own mistakes accepted; but a general
and habitual disagreement of judgment takes away mutual
recognition and respect and renders the tension unhealthy.
What happens is that both those in authority and those under
authority become more concerned with their respective power
over the other than they are with the ultimate objective of
the enterprise in which they are united. Such a society is sick.

The unhealthy tension, then, does not consist merely in the
fact that both authority and those under authority think they
have less freedom and therefore less power than they ought

to have; if both authority and freedom are satisfied with their limitations, then they have become weak. The unhealthy tension consists in a loss of rapport, the replacement of mutual respect by mutual suspicion. Ultimately this means that either authority or freedom has overreached itself, and that the other pole is genuinely hampered in its action. Again, this is a matter of judgment, not of mathematical calculation. Unhealthy tension is probably due as much to personalities as to anything else. Weak persons in authority and strong persons under authority almost automatically mean that internecine strife exists. Yet it is also true that strong persons in authority and weak persons under authority lead to the corruption of freedom and responsibility and the relaxation even of healthy tension. Healthy tension demands strength in both poles. Here it seems worth remarking that a bully is not a strong person. When one reflects long enough on the problems involved, one is tempted to the despairing thesis of anarchy that no man is fit to govern another. The thesis is true to this extent, that no man is fit to govern another unless the one governed accepts the governor; and this acceptance is a free act of consent which cannot be compelled. Acceptance must be merited by the governing officer.

It is at this point that I feel I must modify what Joseph A. Fichter calls "one of the clearest traditions of ecclesiastical administration," the thesis of positional leadership—shared, Fichter points out, with the military and political organizations, but not with the industrial and professional structure.[20] If I read Fichter correctly, I believe he also modifies the thesis more subtly than I am doing it. In the concrete reality of life this distinction between the office and the person is meaningless; and the sustained rationalization which the thesis requires should be imposed on no one. It introduces into the Church that element of depersonalization which may suit the purposes

[20] *Religion as an Occupation* 256–274.

of the military and the political organization, but not the purposes of the Church. It means equivalently that the officer call the subjects not friends but servants, inverting John 15:15. Unless superior and subject reach each other as persons and as fellow-Christians, they are not establishing a Christian relationship. There is no built-in protection of authority which protects against the necessity which lies upon all of fulfilling their responsibility. It is a harsh truth, but it is true that those who cannot win the love and respect of subordinates precisely in the fulfilment of the duty of their office should not be appointed to office, and, if by an honest error they should be appointed, they should neither be retained in it nor wish to retain it.

A healthy tension demands that both authority and freedom assert themselves with vigor; in no other way can the equilibrium be maintained. Here we have to ask whether this is the condition of authority and freedom in the Church. One may say that the principle of tension is not valid in the Church. It has been remarked often enough in the preceding pages that the Church is a unique society with unique forms. But we have also observed that the New Testament does not give the Church the kind of dominative or jurisdictional power which exists in secular societies; and the New Testament speaks quite often of freedom. A brief survey of the New Testament idea of freedom will assist us.

The principle of freedom in the New Testament is the Spirit (2 Corinthians 3:17), or the Son (John 8:36), or the truth (John 8:32). All of these signify a freedom which is other than the freedom which is man's by his nature. This freedom comes from revealed knowledge and from the indwelling Spirit as a principle of life, of thought, and of action. This is the freedom which is not granted by any authority, even by Church authority; this freedom is the radical reality of the new life in Christ—the freedom which is power. Those who have this freedom live as free men, but as servants of God (1 Peter

2:16). It is freedom to righteousness (Romans 6:21), freedom to fulfill the righteousness which Jesus makes possible. It is freedom from sin (Romans 6:18,22), for it is the power to overcome sin. For Paul, in particular, Christian freedom is freedom from the Law (1 Corinthians 10:29; Galatians 2:4, 4:22, 26, and 5:1,13). By a paradox Paul calls the principle which liberates from the law of sin and death the law of the Spirit of life (Romans 8:2), a phrase similar to the paradox of "the perfect law of liberty" (James 1:25). Paul asserts his freedom as an apostle (1 Corinthians 9:1,19).

Freedom from the Law is not to be considered as submission to another law. The Spirit and the truth and the Son replace the Law, but they are not law. Everywhere in the New Testament freedom is conceived as life and action; freedom is not defined as a kind of restraint. The only restraint which the New Testament places upon freedom is love, and love, far from being a restraint of freedom, is the fullness of freedom. The Christian does not act from compulsion or coercion or obligation, but because the power of the Spirit within him is a driving principle of action.

This idea of freedom does not suggest an anarchic Church; we have been at pains to show that the Church is structured in authority. But this unique supernatural freedom, while it is subject to restraint, is not subject to that type of restraint which secular authority employs in secular societies. Christian freedom is restrained by the same principle which confers it, by the Spirit; or, as I have said above, by love. The relations of authority and freedom in the Christian community are determined by love, unless the Christian community wishes to make its decisions on a basis other than the basis which Jesus has established for its decisions. If we are to retain the genuine Christian basis for decision, we cannot think that restraint is imposed only on the freedom of those under authority; authority also is subject to restraint.

Is authority to be restrained only by its own judgment and

virtue? Here we face the problems of structure. The Church
is open to the temptation which threatens any organization
of attributing to structure a sacredness which structure does
not have. Structure is a means to an end, and with the passage
of time and the change of conditions the means can become
inept. The forms of Church authority, we have noticed, have
been frozen at an absolute level reached by a combination of
Renaissance tradition and a defensive posture against modern
attacks on Church authority. The forms of Church offices are
the forms of a princely or a ducal court. It is here that tension
between the theory of authority and the use of authority exists,
for in most modern countries neither the officers of the Church
nor its other members are accustomed to these forms. The
administration is actually not princely or ducal, but it is out
of harmony with the structure when it is not; and if a crisis
comes to pass, authority turns to absolute measures because it
neither knows nor has any other measures—assuming that
authority does not turn to absolute measures because authority
believes in them.

Belief in absolutism does exist, and the belief affects Church
government. We have already noticed that in recent generations the statements of Church officers on obedience and due
submission are numerous; one is hard put to it to find an
official statement on the nature of responsible Christian freedom. The 1960 Statement of the American Bishops was a
splendid exposition of the place which the Catholic ought to
fill in the United States as an adult free responsible citizen of
a republic whose traditions and institutions repose on personal
freedom and which cherishes personal freedom.[21] The statement could easily be adapted to set forth the position of the
Catholic Church. I have no way of knowing whether their
Excellencies considered their statement applicable to the

[21] "On Individual Responsibility," *The Catholic Mind* 59 (1961), 557–
562.

Church or not. We have noticed that the obedience described in official statements is almost always the obedience paid to an absolute ruler by his subject, and that this obedience is neither in theory nor in practice the obedience given in modern democratic states. There can be no solid reason for denying the possibility of evolution in the theory of obedience toward a more democratic idea. Evolution in this direction appears from our survey of the New Testament texts to permit the restoration of some features of the idea and use of authority in the apostolic Church.

In the contemporary forms of Church authority there are effectively no channels through which the authority which resides in the whole Church can normally affect the authority which resides in the officers of the Church. The freedom of the members of the Church is power, but the power has no outlet. The authoritarian structure of the forms of government, however intelligently and justly it may be administered, reflects the concentration of authority and power in the officers. As such, the structure is a practical denial of the authority and power of the faithful. When this concentrated authority is handled with less than perfect prudence and fairness, the consequences can be most unfortunate. Structurally, there is no way to correct abuses of authority except rebellion, and no one thinks rebellion is a good way to do things. If there were regular channels of communication between authority and members, if the authority of the officers normally took pains to see that it reflected the authority of the members, abuses would be much less likely to arise.

These remarks do not imply that we should think of the Church in terms of a parliamentary form, with the bishop acting as a kind of first minister who should resign on a vote of non-confidence. A bishop should not need a parliamentary vote to resign if he knows that he has lost the confidence of his people. Within modern forms how can he ever learn that this has happened? It would be extremely unrealistic to say that it never happens. Church authority, we know, is not conferred by the members of the Church; even when bishops were elected by the faithful of the diocese, the election did not confer authority, but simply designated who should bear it. Of this we are well aware; we are less well aware that Church authority does not confer freedom on the other members of the Church. Modification of the structure would seem to mean at least decentralization of decision, enlarging the scope of action of the individual priest and the individual layman, and broadening considerably the base of policy deliberation. Since the Second Vatican Council opened, there have been numerous suggestions of various councils and commissions which would be channels of expression for the unofficial authority in the Church. These suggestions are at least movements in the right direction, but their success will be very doubtful unless much of the thinking in the Church is changed.

Some recent theological literature deals with the place and authority of the laity in the Church. The major piece in this collection is the massive and carefully reasoned work of Yves Congar.[22] What one misses even in such a study as this is the practical implementation of the function of the layman, admitting that the office of the layman needs a much more thorough theological grounding than it has received. It is my own belief that we shall not know the office and function of the layman until the layman himself, who knows his potentialities and his opportunities better than the clergy do, defines his office and function. When the laity become aware that the decision of what they can do and must do lies with them, they will do it. The lack of real lay leadership is apparent in the very fact that the laity still turn to the clergy for directions on how to lead.

[22] Yves M.-J. Congar, O.P., *Lay People in the Church* (London: Geoffrey Chapman, 1959), translated by Donald Attwater.

Karl Rahner has pointed out three areas in which the laity can make themselves heard now: the Catholic press; Catholic schools; the quality of preaching.[23] In these areas the layman can utter articulate criticism and, once the layman begins to speak, he will find other areas.

Pope Pius XII once spoke of the place of public opinion in the Church. Whatever he may have meant, we have not yet found a way to make public opinion in the Church meaningful. Public opinion in the Church, if it is limited to enthusiastic approval of all hierarchical and pastoral decisions, has as much meaning as an election in Russia. Public opinion is meaningful only when it reviews and, when necessary, criticizes the decisions of authority. Modern democratic processes have shown that public opinion is not a species of insurrection, and that public opinion is quite compatible with a law-abiding and orderly community. Public opinion illustrates a principle which Church officers often forget, that no one ever fights a decision which he thinks he had a part in making. Yet the suggestion that hierarchical and pastoral decisions are subject to review and criticism will seem to many to approach blasphemy. This attitude is as good an example as we can find of the excessive valuation of authority. If authority is not restrained by public opinion, which is the freedom and power of the members of society at work, then what does restrain authority? If we think authority should have no restraint other than self-restraint, then this theoretical position should be clearly stated so that no doubt is left of its meaning. It must be remembered that hierarchical and pastoral decisions have seriously damaged the Church in the past, and we have no guarantee that they will not damage the Church in the future. I cannot say that public opinion would have modified these

[23] Karl Rahner, S.J., *Free Speech in the Church* (New York: Sheed and Ward, 1959) 9–50.

decisions, but it should have had the chance. One can scarcely find such a decision which was not criticized ineffectively by some contemporary.

It should be apparent without argument that public discussion of issues is preferable by far to private and surreptitious discussion. Public discussion of its very nature is not favorable to manifest unfairness, abusive language, and incautious and undocumented assertions. The person who engages in public discussion sticks his neck out, and, if there were free channels of public opinion in the Church, the number who would be willing to enter the arena of discussion would be small. Public discussion creates a weight of opinion which the private representation does not have. One suspects that this is precisely what is wrong with it. The proposal which issues from public discussion has an excellent chance of being pruned of prejudice, and gossip, and unnecessary verbiage and irrelevancies; such a proposal represents the fruit of mature deliberation. I do not know why this type of discussion is thought to tarnish the image of authority. The image of authority is much more tarnished by the uninhibited private sessions in which authority is so often debased. But the officers are not present at these unauthorized grievance meetings. Presumably they do not know what goes on there or, if they do know, they can afford to ignore these desperate little cells.

The absence of regular channels of discussion deprives the Church of a wealth of wisdom and experience in its members. One is sometimes shocked to learn of people who were not consulted in areas in which they had proved themselves masters. Education, carried on under Church auspices, has often been, up to this writing, an outstanding example of failure to consult those who have something to say. Others would adduce other examples. The failure to consult offers no occasion to impute motives; we omit consultation of public opinion because we are not accustomed to consult public opinion. But if the Church is to mobilize its resources for its mission, it must find some way of employing the intelligence and good will of its members other than total control.

It may be unfair to put the question in the form in which I am going to put it, but this risk must be run. Quite simply, the members of the Church are required to show a confidence in the officers of the Church which the officers do not always reciprocate. The members must assume that they, the members, do not share the dedication of the officers to the Church and that they are not responsible adult Catholics. They must assume not only that they are uninformed on the issues with which authority deals—although it is hard to think of any issue which lies entirely beyond them—but also that they are incapable of grasping these issues even if they were informed. In one word, which we have used before, the members must accept authority as paternal in the sense that the members are children incapable of adult responsibility. There may be better ways of destroying communication with adults than treating adults as children, but I cannot think of what these better ways may be. When adults can be trusted only to obey without question, they are not being trusted at all. Over-valuation of authority is under-valuation of those who are subject to authority.

Our structural problem can be neatly summarized thus: we must under present forms await the decision of authority for any modification in the structure. The great change initiated by John XXIII is that he invited public discussion of such problems. But if a modification of structure is conceived as a grant of greater freedom and responsibility to the members of the Church, nothing will have been changed. Real change means that authority in the Church recognizes the power and authority which belong to the faithful by the constitution of the Church, not by pontifical largesse. Real change means that the forms and structure reflect the reality of the Church, not the reality of the duchy or The Organization. Real change is real only if it is the work of the whole Church and not exclusively the work of the officers. But the initiative still lies with the officers. We shall know that a change has been made when the initiative no longer lies there. *The Constitution on the Church* provides that the laity should reveal their needs and their desires to their pastors, and under proper conditions should express their opinions on those things that concern the good of the Church.[24] These expressions should be uttered through the organs erected by the Church for this purpose. Such organs do not yet exist except in a few dioceses in an inchoative stage. Certainly one of the first areas in which the laity can be active is in the erection of such organs. The explicit provision for such organs is an important step away from the princely and the ducal forms.

[24] Butler and Baum, *op. cit.*, chapter IV, #37.

14. The Mystery of Authority

THERE IS A FINAL CONSIDERATION of authority in the Church which we cannot omit. We have said often enough that the Church is a unique society with a unique end and that the Church cannot use the means proper to secular societies. When we think of authority in the Church, we must not treat authority as if it lay outside the mystery of the Church. For the Church is a mystery, and authority is also involved in the mystery. Many mistakes are made because Church authority is treated as if it were like any other authority and, therefore, without mystery, open to analysis.

In theological language mystery designates a reality which is beyond comprehension. A mystery is beyond comprehension because it is a revelation of God in some way or another, either of the personal reality of God or of his actions, in particular his saving acts. We see that the Church is a revelation both of the personal reality of God, because it is the body of Christ, and of the saving act of God, because it is the extension of the Incarnation. But we have elements in the Church which are not identified with the revealed mystery, and we treat these elements as rationally comprehensible. The church building is erected by architects, engineers, and building trade workers. When the parish pays its bills, the parish pays them in the same currency which everyone else uses. And it might appear that church administration, like church construction and church finances, does not have anything mysterious about it; we use the techniques which are used everywhere for these purposes.

It has been the purpose of this entire study to show that the use of authority in the Church cannot be the same as the use of secular authority. This proposition is based on the idea of authority found in the New Testament. According to the New Testament, authority is one of the constitutive elements of the Church, and thus authority shares the mysterious reality of the Church in a way in which buildings and accounts do not. The New Testament idea of Church authority is explicitly different from the known idea of authority in other organizations. The true nature of Church authority cannot be discovered by a purely rational analysis; and a purely rational analysis is not intended in this writing. Conclusions drawn from a philosophical conception of authority have of themselves no application whatever to the authority of the Church.

The mysterious reality is not grasped by reason, but accepted by faith; any thinking which we do with the hope of penetrating the reality more deeply rises from faith and is governed by faith. In all theological reasoning the danger of rationalism is always present. It would not be too grossly simplified to say that all heresies ultimately were efforts to reduce the mystery to something reasonable. Not all rationalism issues in formal heresy or even in material heresy; but the normal and expected issue of rationalism is theological error, a misconception of the mystery which may be no less damaging because it falls short of full and formal heresy. Authority in the Church may be one of the points where rationalism is more subtle. Of theological interpretations of authority one may say that if they leave Church authority entirely comprehensible, they fail to present its reality.

We locate the mystery of Church authority in the fact that it is an authority whose power is the power of love. This love is the love revealed in the person and teaching of Jesus, that unique love which we call Christian. The nature of Christian love is known by the revelation of God in Christ, and the capacity of Christian love is based not on nature, but on the life communicated by the indwelling Spirit. When Church authority uses any other power than the power of love, it ceases to exhibit its distinctively Christian and ecclesial nature. This conception of authority can be apprehended only by faith; and only by Christian hope can we be assured that such authority can be effective. The prudence and wisdom of human experience suggest that such authority will have no genuine power, that authority will be helpless, that the society governed by such authority will degenerate into anarchy.

The end and purpose of Church authority likewise is apprehended only by faith. Human societies have an end which can be weighed and measured, and the success with which the end is achieved can be defined. How is the Church to define her success in achieving her end? She has no way of knowing how much she has achieved; she can only know that she loves. If the success of the Church is measured by such statistical data as the number of communicants, the number, size and distribution of churches, schools and other institutions, and her financial solvency, the attainment of the end of the Church is not known at all. Only faith assures us that the end of the Church can be as well attained without these things as with them, although this does not dispense us from making as much use of these means as we can.

Precisely with reference to authority, the common measure of success is the presence of order and discipline. Order and discipline do not attest that the Church is attaining her end. Where the Church suffers from disorder and lack of discipline, she is failing in her mission. But if authority restores discipline, authority does not thereby guarantee the success of the Church. If Church order and discipline were as well regulated as the discipline of an army, a prison, or a manufacturing establishment, we should still be ignorant of whether the Church is accomplishing her work. To impose alien forms upon her does not assure her success, and some alien forms appear to be in opposition to her mission.

It may be urged that, in repeating that the Church must find her own style of order and discipline, I am not presenting any constructive suggestions. This I admit, but I do not believe that a complete program of discipline is within my powers to produce or within the powers of any single person. A truly ecclesiastical discipline will be produced by the total wisdom and experience of the Church enlightened by faith. Such a discipline, we have seen, is a discipline of love. It means a union of wills in consent achieved by what is called a shared decision. Consent is given, based on an intelligent perception of what is to be done. Inevitable doubts are resolved by candid discussion and communication of information, and, most of all, because mutual confidence exists among all those who are engaged in the action. I do not believe such an atmosphere can be created by the mere dominative use of authority.

As a mystery, we said, Church authority must be accepted by faith. It has not been sufficiently noticed in theological and ascetical literature that those who hold authority as well as those who are subject to authority must accept authority by faith. There is no lack of explanations of obedience based on faith and of exhortations to this virtue. There is not a corresponding abundance of explanations of the use of authority based on faith and of exhortations to this type of government. Authority must be accepted as that unique power which Jesus gave to his Church. Authority must be accepted with the assurance that this unique power is sufficient for the purpose of the Church. The assent of faith in the true nature of Church authority is the only protection the Church has against the corruption of authority by secularization and the conversion of authority into a power structure. Faith is the only protection against the adaptation of Church authority to the personal ends of those who hold authority.

If faith is required in the acceptance of authority, faith is equally necessary in the use of authority. Sound theory, we have noticed, does not always result in sound practice. The temptations to compromise Church authority by the use of means unsuited to Church authority are many. The number of occasions when it appears that a display of power will settle matters is apparently unlimited. A display of power will usually settle matters; it can and often does at the same time destroy the Christian rapport between authority and its subjects. The way of leadership in love is far more difficult and demanding, and the immediate results are often less impressive than the results achieved by a show of power. But the Church has always maintained the principle that good results achieved by the wrong means are not good results.

It is scarcely possible to catalogue a list of ways in which Church authority can fail to make decisions by faith. Such a list would sound very much like a list of complaints; it would certainly be incomplete, and it would not be positive. It has been our purpose to avoid the negative and the complaining tone, in spite of the fact that we thus deprive our study of some piquant and anecdotal features. But the matter is too serious for mere wit. Authority in the Church, we have said more than once, is the concern of all the members of the Church. It is not possible for any member of the Church, even for any officer, to prescribe in detail a method of making decisions in faith; and such a prescription would most inappropriately be made by one who has no experience in the decisions of authority.

But officers are not the only members of the Church who

must make decisions based on faith. This principle governs the life of every Christian. Hence the individual member of the Church can often tell when a decision is based on something other than faith. The individual member is not deceived when he is told that he does not know all the issues involved. Knowledge of all the issues is not always necessary to discern when faith is being compromised. It can happen that the individual member, just because he is personally less involved in the decision and has nothing in particular to defend, can have an insight into the issues which those concerned do not have. And this leads us into a theme which has been stated earlier. Authority can protect itself against decisions made without faith by consulting the Church.

A decision made with the consultation of the Church is itself an act of faith in the presence and power of the Spirit in the Church. If we doubt that the Spirit speaks through the general membership of the Church, we give cause for concern as to what we think the Church is. That such consultation seems to involve clumsy processes may be true; but actually we do not know what the processes might be, because processes for such consultation scarcely exist. We are driven back once again to the question of public opinion in the Church. In the modern democratic state no politician can afford to be ignorant of public opinion on public issues. If the politician pays no attention to public opinion, the electorate will reject him as its representative. In the Church those who bear office hold the office without responsibility to an electorate; this does not mean that they are not responsible to the Church. Church officers have an even more powerful motive for attending to public opinion. Public opinion in the Church is one of the channels through which the Spirit speaks.

Are the officers of the Church, however, representatives of the people of the Church? An unqualified negative answer to this question seems impossible. The officers are not elected representatives in the political sense, nor do they have a popular mandate. Apart from these features, Church authority seems to deserve fully the title of representative. For the union between officers and people in the Church is an element of the mystery of the Church. It is a union of love, and it scarcely deserves to be called a union of love unless it is a union of intent and purpose. If the harmony of this union is achieved solely by the imposition of superior wills on inferior wills, we should find another name for the union than love; for love means mutual and not unilateral agreement. In a sense far more profound than in democratic constitutions, authority in the Church must be supported by the free consent of those whom it governs. There is an irremovable opposition between love and constraint.

This element of the mystery is surely the most difficult to incorporate into practice. There are so many other ways in which authority can make decisions, all of them recommended by good political, or military, or commercial experience, all much quicker and more expeditious, and all protecting authority from the need of humbling itself before those whom it governs—that is, from adopting the attitude recommended by Jesus in the gospels. All of these ways achieve the end of The Organization more surely than the way of the mystery can achieve it; all these ways fail to achieve what the way of the mystery achieves, the fulfillment of each person in the Church. All of these ways are ways of securing the Church by securing the authority of the Church rather than by securing the whole membership; and all these ways imply that if authority is secure, the Church is secure. All these ways seek to make the condition of the Church independent of the love shown by Church authority and Church members; and for this reason all these ways fail most ignominiously where they succeed most brilliantly.

Faith in Christ means faith in the whole Christ, and this

includes faith in the Church which is the body of Christ. Lacking this faith, authority may have faith only in itself; and if authority has no more faith than this, authority will have no more strength than it has in itself. Authority will be more and more compelled to fortify its position by the kind of power which is alien to the Church. It will pay by the loss of love for each bit of strength which it gains. Authority can cut itself off from the resources of life and of power with which Jesus has endowed the Church and from the fullness of the Spirit which dwells in the Church. For authority is a member of the body, and it needs the fullness of the body if it is to reach its own proper fullness.

*   *   *   *

No one, I trust, will conclude from the preceding pages that I think authority in the Church is an easy function to fulfill. On the contrary, it is painfully evident that one of the ways in which the Church suffers is poverty of the kind of person who can bear authority in the Church worthily. Jesus himself sought for twelve such, and found only eleven. The charge of authority demands the fullness of the Christian life in those who bear authority; but the fullness of the Christian life is not present there any more than it is present in the Church at large. The Church has more offices than she has men to fill them. And this is very near the heart of the mystery, that the Church seems doomed to perform her mission with inadequate means. Authority has often been her ignominy and shame, her cross and passion.

Let no one think that the officers of the Church bear all the blame for the failures of the Church. At the same time, the officers must bear their share with the faithful. If the officers have failed to show themselves the lackeys and slaves of others, the faithful have been no more prompt to assume the position of lackeys and slaves. If the officers have failed to draw strength from the whole Church, the faithful have refused to strengthen the officers by the means which they have in their power. The chilling of love and the loss of mutual understanding are the work both of the officers and of the faithful. Neither the officers nor those who are subject to authority have been willing to accept the fact just stated, that officers are often inadequate to the trust committed to them. And there seems to be no way to evade this fact; it is too constant in the history of the Church.

How the Church rises above this inadequacy in its officers is again a part of the mystery. But the Church certainly rises above it when authority, conscious of its inadequacy, seeks strength in the only place where it can find strength—in the whole Church. The Church rises above inadequacy when the faithful respond to the request for strength by bearing and forgiving, by tolerance of weakness and error to seventy times seven, by preserving their own Christian integrity, by rising above their own limitations, by not allowing the inadequacy of their officers to become an excuse for withholding love. The Church rises above her humanity when both officers and members cherish the divine element in her, which is the surpassing love diffused by the Spirit. When authority and members are united in this love, human error and human malice cannot have their full consequences. How this is accomplished is the mystery of the Church. Authority and obedience are not enough.

No genuine member of the Church is unwilling to render to those who bear authority all the assistance which lies within his power. He will render it all the more readily when it is sought and welcomed. Ecclesiastical superiors and their subjects will profit when both are ready to apologize for their error and weakness, and to acknowledge guilt even publicly in terms more particular than the *Confiteor*. The Second

Vatican Council has prepared a scheme in which the Church confesses its guilt for its own share in the unhappy schism of the Reformation. This splendid example should show that authority does not lose prestige by acknowledging its faults, and it can be followed for events much more recent than the Protestant Reformation. In the Church the image should never arise of an authority which can do no wrong and commit no offense. The faithful are not moved to communicate strength to an authority which they believe needs no strength from them.

Our conclusion is not cynical acceptance of the fact of our inadequacy. Nor is our conclusion contentment with the mediocre and a timid policy of striving for the possible; this policy is politics by definition. Our conclusion should be a renewed insight into the truth that the Church has no power except the power of God, and he has revealed that this power is love. We have the resources to do what we must, but we have not always looked for these resources where they can be found. Jesus prayed that all should be one as he and the Father are one. We usually think of his prayer in terms of the reunion of dissident Christians. We need to think of it in terms of the relations between authority in the Church and the other members. Because the Church is a community of men the unity of authority and members will never be perfect. This is scarcely a decent excuse for organizing the structure of the Church in ways which are calculated, as far as human planning and diligence can manage it, to keep the unity of officers and members imperfect.